Niccolò Machiavelli's
THE
PRINCE
and The Discourses

ROBERT SOBEL
ASSISTANT PROFESSOR OF HISTORY
HOFSTRA UNIVERSITY

Simon & Schuster, Inc.
15 Columbus Circle
New York, NY 10023

Monarch and colophons are trademarks
of Simon & Schuster, registered in the
U.S. Patent and Trademark Office.

ISBN: 0-671-00565-0

Library of Congress Catalog Card Number: 66-1794

Printed in the United States of America

TABLE OF CONTENTS

Introduction   5

The Prince 11

The Discourses 56

Other Works and Later Life 60

Contrasting Views on Machiavelli 63

Sample Essay Questions 68

Bibliography 75

INTRODUCTION

THE WORLD OF MACHIAVELLI. The period from the middle of the fourteenth century to the middle of the sixteenth century is usually termed the Renaissance by historians. The word means "rebirth," and was coined by nineteenth century writers who saw in the intellectual life of Europe in this period a startling contrast to what had gone before. Whereas the Middle Ages was viewed as a time of religious stress on the next life, the Renaissance was considered a time during which intellectuals had worldly interests. The Medieval man was viewed as little more than one unit in the all-encompassing confines of the Catholic Church, while the man of the Renaissance prized individualism over all else. The man of 1200 was thought to be interested in storing up good works, so as to enjoy paradise; the man of 1500 was more interested in gaining gold and power to enjoy the here and now.

We know now that these distinctions are overstated at best and gross exaggerations at worst. The attributes of the Renaissance were present in Europe throughout the Middle Ages, and grew in intensity from the end of the Norse invasions of the tenth and eleventh centuries to the sixteenth. One can scarcely say, then, that the Renaissance was the rebirth of the classical heritage, for that heritage never truly died. It may be said, however, that this period saw the acceleration and fruition of tendencies already present in Europe. Among the more important of these were: the growth of secularism, which is to say the growth in importance of worldly interests; the development of humanism, an intellectual movement that stressed enjoyment of all aspects of life, and especially of the ideas and values of pre-Christian civilizations, such as those of Greece and Rome; the interest in individualism, including stress on man as an end in himself, rather than as merely one cog in the vast machine of the Church. The typical Renaissance man, then, was interested in all things, enjoyed life, strove for worldly acclaim and wealth, and had a deep interest in classical civilizations. Such a man was Machiavelli.

Although the Renaissance spirit infiltrated most parts of Europe, it was strongest in Italy. There, a worldly Papacy acted as patron of the arts; wealthy leaders of city-states attempted to wrench power from their neighbors; middle-class merchants, made wealthy during the Crusades, attempted to become worldly themselves, or failing at that, patronized other worldly men. In Italy, too, the classical spirit was strong; it had never died, even during the period of the Dark Ages. Change was in the air, and with it, the opportunity for power and wealth. Venice, the strongest of the city-states, had great economic power, which it attempted to translate into political control of Italy. The Sforza family of Milan had similar aspirations, as did the Aragonese rulers of Naples. The Papal States, commanding both spiritual and economic power, and the crafty and influential Medicis of Florence, thought along similar lines. Each would willingly sacrifice the others for gold and power.

Shortly before Columbus discovered America, Florence and Naples concluded a secret alliance against Milan. The Sforzas learned of this, and appealed to King Charles VIII of France for aid. In 1494, Charles invaded Italy, initiating a series of wars that did not end until 1559. Charles succeeded in driving the Medicis out of Florence. In their place, Savonarola, a Dominican monk who opposed the worldliness of the Renaissance, ruled with an iron fist. Savonarola dreamed of a unified Italy, but could do little about it; he was killed in 1498, after Charles had died and the merchant aristocrats returned to the city. In 1512, Pope Julius II drove the French from Italy. Florence, which had an alliance with France, was retaken by the Medicis, who punished the republican leaders of the city with death or exile. One of those exiled was Niccolò Machiavelli, then a 43-year-old bureaucrat in the employ of the pro-French Florentines.

THE LIFE OF MACHIAVELLI. Niccolò Machiavelli was born in 1469. His father was a Florentine lawyer and civil servant, who was wealthy enough to provide his son with an adequate education of a classical nature, but lacked the proper connections to gain young Niccolò an important government post when the son showed an interest in government. To further complicate matters, the Machiavellis had a record of opposition to the Medicis. One of Niccolò's ancestors had been imprisoned for life as a result of his conflicts with the Medici bankers. Niccolò's father was apparently a supporter of the republic, which in those days and that place meant that he favored political control by a group of the state's leading citizens. This alone assured both father and son a shaky position under the Medicis, who wished to establish a monarchy in Florence.

Machiavelli grew up during a period of Medici power. Cosimo de Medici gained control of the city in 1434, and ruled it until his death in 1464, four years before Machiavelli's birth. He was succeeded by Piero the Gouty, who held power for five years. In 1469, control fell to Giuliano and Lorenzo de Medici. In 1478, rival families united in an assassination attempt on both men. Giuliano was killed, but Lorenzo escaped with minor wounds. He recovered, punished his enemies, consolidated his power, and ruled until 1492, when he was succeeded by Piero de Medici. It was Piero who was ousted by Charles VIII in 1494.

The period of Lorenzo's power has sometimes been called the Augustan Age of the Italian Renaissance, or the Age of Lorenzo. The ruler himself was referred to as Lorenzo the Magnificent. He managed to juggle the uneasy alliance of Italian cities with skill, and effectively neutralized the power of France. While doing this, he also wrote poetry and dabbled in painting, and gathered around him men interested in the arts and letters. Thus, the young Machiavelli grew up during the height of the Italian Renaissance, and in its most important city. Although far from the seats of power because of his family's politics, he might have known or at least seen such great figures as Leonardo da Vinci, Botticelli, Ghiberti, and Brunelleschi.

Michelangelo was born six years after Machiavelli and Titian eight years after. Yet, despite the fact that he lived at a time and in a place where there was more genius per square mile than at any time since the Periclean Age of Athens, Machiavelli appears to have been uninterested in the arts; he scarcely mentions them in his works. Further, although he was 23 years old at the time of the first voyage to America, he scarcely took note of it, and certainly did not begin to realize its implications. Machiavelli was interested in his city, Italy, and the forces that directly affected both. Little else seemed to catch his eye.

Machiavelli was 25 when Charles VIII invaded Florence, and 29 when Savonarola was burned at the stake. The young man observed both Charles and Savonarola and, as we have discovered from his writings, carefully considered the reasons for their successes and failures. At the same time, he must have been involved in the movements to restore Florence to republican rule. Otherwise, he would not have been so amply rewarded when, after the death of Savonarola, the merchant aristocrats regained control of the city. At that time Machiavelli was named to the important post of Chancellor of the Second Chancery and member of the Council of Ten of Liberty and Peace. In the former post, he was given control over foreign and military affairs, and in the latter, was one of the administrators of Florence. In these posts, he acted as one of the half dozen or so most important men of the city.

Machiavelli served in several special diplomatic assignments, and the reports he sent back to Florence show that he learned his craft well. In these years, his vision and scope expanded from Florence to all of western Europe. In reading his diplomatic reports, one can sense Machiavelli's intense interests in the question of true power as opposed to appearances. His missions took him to the courts of Emperor Maximilian of the Holy Roman Empire and King Louis XII of France. Most important, he visited many of the other Italian city-states, and learned of their internal politics and court intrigues.

While in Rome, Machiavelli may have had conversations with Cesare Borgia, the brilliant, unscrupulous, and underhanded son of Rodrigo Borgia, who was then Pope Alexander VI. The son took after the father; at that time, the Pope was attempting to gain control of all of Italy. In this drive, his son Cesare was his major ally. Cesare destroyed the Orsini and Colonna families of Rome, who had challenged Borgia power. He then turned northward to Romagna, in this way flanking Machiavelli's city of Florence. Cesare destroyed most of the rulers of this region and, in 1501, became Duke of Romagna. These conquests were accomplished through the use of military force, diplomacy, intrigue, and dissimulation. His sister, Lucrezia, was as important as his army in this campaign. She married three princes of desirable territories, then participated in their murders, all to further the Borgia ambitions.

Cesare turned to the south in 1501. He formed an alliance with France and turned on Naples. At this point, his fortunes took a turn for the worse. Revolts broke out in some of the conquered areas, and although they were put down, dissension remained. In 1503, his father died, and the new Pope Julius II, was hostile to the Borgias. Forming his own armies, the Pope conquered much of central Italy and displaced Cesare as the major political force in Italy. Cesare responded by entering into an alliance with Spain, but Julius pressed on. In 1509, Cesare was arrested at Naples and sent to Spain, where he died the following year.

During this period, Machiavelli watched Cesare carefully, noting his successes and failures, and analyzing the reasons for both. At the same time, he took care to advance his own fortunes. He became personal advisor to Pietro Soderini, who was Gonfalonier (a high civil servant) of Florence from 1502 to 1512.

During this period, Florence was allied with France against Spain, some German states, and Italian forces of the League of Mantua. Realizing that Florence was weak, and could not count on France for substantial aid, Machiavelli urged the military reorganization of the Florentine militia and the establishment of a civilian armed force. This force won a significant victory in 1508-9, when it took Pisa after a seige. In 1512, it was crushed, however, as a Spanish-German-Italian force, with the Medici enemies of the Florentine republic in the van, conquered the home city of Machiavelli. Rightly believing that all supporters of the republic would be punished by Lorenzo de Medici, grandson of Lorenzo the Magnificent, the Florentines welcomed the new prince, expelled the republican leaders, and placed some of them in irons. Machiavelli himself was arrested for treason, and underwent tortures before being released and allowed to go into exile. He returned to his family's home near San Casciano in Tuscany. Since Lorenzo and his allies were firmly in power, Machiavelli must have realized that, at the age of 43, his public life had drawn to an end.

Still, he could not but hope to return to the seats of power. Since he could not return as a republican ally of the merchant aristocrats who opposed Lorenzo, it would have to be done as an ally of the Medicis. Machiavelli's terms of exile forbade him to return to Florence, but his words might act for him. Thus, he became an author. From 1512 until his death in 1527, he wrote several important works, of which *The Prince* and *The Discourses on the First Ten Books of Titus Livius* are the most important. Other books were *The Art of War* and *The History of Florence*. He also wrote a play, *Mandragola*, several short sketches, and some poetry. Of these, *The Prince* has emerged as the classic work on political power, while *The Discourses*, though not read as often or as carefully, is considered the most complete statement of Machiavelli's philosophy.

THE PRINCE. If the major reason for Machiavelli's career as a writer was that of returning him to power, the second most important factor in his literary efforts was that of boredom. After a life spent in the most cultured cities of the Renaissance and among the most powerful people of his time, Machiavelli, still a young man, found himself condemned to live among peasants, woodsmen, and country priests, who were illiterate at worst and unsophisticated at best. In a letter to Vettori, the Florentine ambassador at Rome, he wrote of his life: "I am living in the country since my disgrace. I get up at dawn and go to the little wood where I see what work has been done." Then Machiavelli describes his mornings: after reading some poetry on the side of a hill, he would have his mid-day meal. Then to the village inn, where he would talk to the local butcher and miller. This once-mighty and highly intellectual leader of men would spend the next few hours "with these boors playing cards or dice; we quarrel over farthings." With relief, he would leave them in the early evening, and return home to his true friends. He writes:

> Before I enter [my study] I take off my rough mud-stained country dress. I put on my royal and curial robes, and enter, decently dressed, the ancient courts of men of old, where I am welcomed kindly and fed on that fare which is mine alone, and for which I was born: where I am not ashamed to address them and ask them for the reasons for their action, and they reply considerately. For two hours I forget all my cares. I know no more trouble, death loses its terrors. I am utterly translated in their company. And since Dante says that we can never attain knowledge unless we retain what we hear, I have noted down the capital I have accumulated from their conversation and composed a little book, *The Prince*, in which I probe as deeply as I can the consideration of this subject, discussing what a principality is, the variety of such states, how they are won, how they are held, how they are lost.

This, then, is the background for the writing of *The Prince*. Here we have a man in his mid-forties, who is attuned to the tempos of his time, knows the workings of states, and is interested in the motivations of men. He had been close to the seats of power, and, although a republican, admired Cesare Borgia and Julius II. He was a strong believer in the glories of Florence, but felt even stronger the need for the unification of Italy. Cesare Borgia failed in his attempt to unite the nation, and Julius seemed interested in other matters. At the head of his old city was Lorenzo de Medici, grandson of Lorenzo the Magnificent. Here was the perfect candidate for the role of unifier of Italy. Machiavelli was bored in

San Casciano; he yearned to return to Florence. If Lorenzo could be made to realize Machiavelli's importance, perhaps the exile would be rescinded. Thus, Machiavelli retired to his study and, surrounded by the works of the great classical authors, composed *The Prince,* which he dedicated to Lorenzo, and, in order both to flatter him and recall past glories, referred to him as Lorenzo the Magnicent. Historians doubt whether Lorenzo ever read the document; in any case, he died in 1519 without ever having been in touch with Machiavelli. *The Prince* was read by others, however, and was finally published in 1532, five years after its author's death.

THE PRiNCE

DEDICATION

Machiavelli notes that anyone who hopes to gain the favor of a prince must present him with a gift. This book is his gift to Lorenzo de Medici. As was the custom, Machiavelli depreciates the book, saying it is unworthy of acceptance. Still, it may prove useful. The author has been close to the seats of power, and has learned how princes gain and lose control of situations and people. He likens himself to a humble landscape painter who surveys the scene from all angles before putting it down on canvas. The Prince must act in the same way; he must "know thoroughly the nature of people" and the people must know him. In this way, the book may prove useful, and may enable Lorenzo to attain the grandeur and good fortune that could be his. Machiavelli is not uninterested in his own fate. If Lorenzo finds the work useful, he may "gaze down from the summit of [his] lofty position toward this humble spot, [he] will recognize the great and unmerited sufferings inflicted on me by a cruel fate."

COMMENT: Beneath the flowery phrases of this standard introduction, Machiavelli is seen trying to strike a bargain with Lorenzo. In order to reinforce this offer of an alliance, Machiavelli repeats it in somewhat different terms in the last chapter of the book. In essence, he is saying that Lorenzo views the world from the summit of power, while Machiavelli sees it from the base of the mountain. Lorenzo has the position that may enable him to become powerful, but lacks much needed information. Machiavelli has the information, but lacks the position. One might say they were made for one another. Thus, he suggests that they pool their resources. This is not stated outright for two reasons. In the first place, the style of the Renaissance called for roundabout statements. In addition, Machiavelli himself and his family before him had been enemies of the Medicis. He could scarcely allude to his experience in this role, or his positions of trust in previous Florentine governments.

CHAPTERS I AND II

There are two kinds of states: republics and monarchies. The latter can further be subdivided into two groups: those that are hereditary and have been under the same family for many years, and newly-established ones, which have been acquired through war or good fortune. The author will not concern himself with republics, since he dealt with them elsewhere (Machiavelli is referring to his *History of Florence*). Instead, he will dwell on monarchies. Hereditary states are easier to maintain than newly-established ones; the people, once used to rule, will not want to change it. Even if deposed, the Prince of a hereditary monarchy may be able to regain his post without much difficulty. The author notes that the

Duke of Ferrara was able to withstand the attacks of Venice and
even Pope Julius, primarily because the people of Ferrara were
accustomed to his rule, and rallied to his cause. Another reason
for this affection was the Duke's support of the status quo, which
the author implies most people want to maintain. Machiavelli notes,
however, that once changes are begun and the people become accustomed to them, others will follow.

> **COMMENT:** These chapters, and the nine that follow, are
> devoted to an analysis of the various kinds of monarchies.
> Machiavelli will open this section with familiar and contem-
> porary examples, study the great figures of antiquity, then
> return to Cesare Borgia, who may be considered the hero
> of this section. He implies that Lorenzo may profit from
> Cesare's example.

CHAPTER III

Princes of newly-established monarchies face two major difficulties:
(1) since men change masters willingly in the hope of bettering
themselves, they may continue to fight after the new Prince wishes
them to stop. This may be done because the revolters, rising up
to better themselves, may wind up in a worse situation. (2) the
new Prince finds himself opposed by both his followers and his
opponents. Machiavelli observes that King Louis XII of France
could not hold Milan because of local opposition to his rule. When
the old prince, Duke Ludovico, reappeared on the frontier, Louis
was forced to withdraw.

It is much easier to control an area which is recaptured. The Prince,
on returning to the city, knows why he was forced out the first
time, and who among the population had opposed him. He may
correct the first and eliminate the second. Machiavelli notes that
when Louis returned to Milan, he was able to remain firmly in
the saddle. Similar situations are cited from the histories of Burgundy, Brittany, Gascony, and Normandy. The author concludes
that the new Prince must keep two things in mind: (1) the old
Prince and his family must be made "extinct"; (2) the new Prince
must not make changes either in laws or taxes.

What if the Prince captures lands that have radically different
customs, languages, and laws from those of his original state? Such
a situation existed when the Turks captured Greece. In such a
case, Machiavelli recommends that the Prince take up residence in
the conquered areas. "Being on the spot, disorders can be seen as
they arise and can quickly be remedied." In addition, the Prince
can make sure his officials are not cheating him. The conquered
peoples will be more loyal if the Prince resides among them, and
rivals will be less likely to attack. If the Prince cannot live among
his newly-conquered subjects, he must then either maintain a
large army among them or plant colonies of inhabitants from his

old domain. Machiavelli thinks the second alternative is preferable to the first; "the colonies will cost the Prince little; with little or no expense on his part, he can send and maintain them; he only injures those whose lands and houses are taken to give to the new inhabitants, and these form but a small proportion of the state."

Once established in power, the Prince should become the leader and defender of his less powerful neighbors. Then, when the neighboring states are endangered, he will be invited to intervene in their affairs. He will find natural allies among the opponents of the regime. If the Prince is careful not to take too much power too rapidly, and governs well, the neighboring state will fall into his hands easily. Machiavelli then notes that this was the way the Romans took many new lands. Returning to his own experience, he describes the methods by which Louis of France took parts of Italy. He was called to Italy by Venice, and the two powers combined to capture Lombardy. Then many other Italian states sought his friendship. If Louis had then followed the advice offered by Machiavelli, he would have had little difficulty in maintaining his power in Italy. Instead of being moderate in his approaches and attempting to retain his allies, the King set off to new adventures. Louis helped the Pope occupy Romagna. By doing this, he frightened those friendly states allied to him who were fearful of the Papacy, and at the same time helped create a potential rival.

Louis then compounded his error by going to Italy himself to prevent Pope Alexander from becoming ruler of Tuscany; now the Pope mistrusted him as well. Finally, he divided Naples with Spain, angering the city's inhabitants and bringing to Italy another strong potential rival. Machiavelli approves of Louis' desires for power, but notes that he made five major mistakes: (1) he crushed the smaller powers instead of using them to increase his control; (2) he increased the power of one state (the Pope's) instead of keeping it subservient to himself; (3) he himself had brought a rival, Spain, into the picture, when it was not necessary or desirable; (4) Louis had not come to Italy to live, thus displeasing the Italians; (5) he had not established colonies in Italy, having failed to reside there himself. Still, disaster might have been avoided if Louis had not made still a sixth mistake: that of taking territory from Venice. Once Venice lost hopes of a strong French alliance, it could no longer be trusted to protect Louis' flanks from his enemies.

Machiavelli then deals with objections to his proposals. It was argued that Louis yielded Romagna to Alexander and Naples to Spain (actions that angered Venice) to avoid war with these powers. Machiavelli replies that "one ought never to allow a disorder to take place in order to avoid war. War is not thereby avoided, but only deferred to your disadvantage." Other critics of Machiavelli argued that Louis gave in to the Pope in return for promises of the cardinalship of Rohan and the dissolution of his marriage. Machiavelli replies that the word of princes must be suspect; never give up something concrete for promises of future favors. He then notes, and also shows his national sentiments, that the French Cardinal Rohan once told him "that the Italians do not understand war." Machiavelli responded by saying "that the French do not understand politics, for if they did, they would never allow the Church to become so great. And experience has shown us that the greatness in Italy of the Church and also of Spain has been caused by France, and her ruin has proceeded from them." From this, Machiavelli formulates a general rule: "Whoever is the cause of another becoming powerful, is ruined himself." To make another person powerful, you must use "either craft or force," and the person who has benefited by your work will not trust you, for then he will know how crafty and forceful you can be.

COMMENT: This is one of the most contentious chapters in the book. It appears as though Machiavelli is drawing a blueprint for a foreign invasion of Italy. He implies that if a future invader avoids the mistakes of King Louis, he will be able to capture and control Italy. On the other hand, Machiavelli was an Italian nationalist, and was writing his book in the hope of persuading Lorenzo to unite Italy under the banner of Florence. Why, then, tell foreigners the secrets of success? Some critics argue that this view of Chapter III is a misreading. Instead of concentrating on the second part of the chapter, Lorenzo was to have considered the first. There Machiavelli states that Louis was strong in Milan, Burgundy, Brittany, Gascony, and Normandy precisely because he had done the right things there, and had failed in Italy because he ignored the dictums put forth by Machiavelli. Lorenzo, who knew the history of Italy, would have realized that Cesare, in taking most of central Italy, followed the type of advice offered by Machiavelli. Then, when he formed an alliance with France to conquer the South, he failed, for the same reason that Louis failed in Italy: that of bringing a strong ally to the scene, which disrupted previously contented subjects. Thus, Machiavelli is not trying in Chapter III to show foreigners how to capture Italy, but rather encouraging Lorenzo to follow the examples of Cesare Borgia in central Italy and Louis in France, and avoid their mistakes in southern Italy and, in the case of Louis, in the invasions of Italy. If this is done, Lorenzo's unified Italy will be as strong as France. Then, Machiavelli seems to imply, he can invade and capture France, scrupulously avoiding Louis' mistakes in Italy. This may be done for, as he said to Cardinal Rohan, "the French do not understand politics."

CHAPTER IV

In this chapter, Machiavelli discusses the reasons why Alexander the Great's empire did not erupt into rebellions after his death. He notes that kingdoms are governed in two ways: (1) by the Prince and his ministers; (2) by the Prince and barons, who hold power independently. The barons have states of their own, and thus the inhabitants of the kingdom have a dual loyalty: to their Prince and to their baron. Turkey is an example of the first type of government. It is ruled by a single monarch, whose ministers are given responsibilities over various provinces, but have no power in their own right. In France, we have an example of the second type of kingdom. The nobles are recognized as special individuals by their subjects, who love them. Machiavelli observes that it would be difficult for a single Prince to conquer Turkey, but once it was taken, it would be easy to rule. By this he means that the monarch would be powerful and difficult to dislodge, in part because his subjects were all loyal to a single individual. On the other hand, once he was replaced, the new ruler could easily gain the loyalty of a people used to following a single man. France would be easy to conquer but difficult to rule because the divided ruler and barons would not be able to present a unified front against the invader. However, the new ruler would find it most difficult to command the loyalties of a people used to divided sovereignty.

The author then looks at the government of Darius of Persia when it was conquered by Alexander. He notes that it was similar to that of Turkey, and as a result, after it was conquered, remained loyal to Alexander. Had Alexander's successors remained united instead of squabbling among themselves, there would have been no problems with Persia. On the other hand, the Romans were unable to prevent constant rebellions in their Greek, French, and Spanish provinces. These were taken with comparative ease because they were not united. This lack of centralized power militated against peaceful control. In addition, "when the Romans fell out among themselves, any one of them could count on the support of that part of the province where he had established authority."

COMMENT: In this chapter, Machiavelli is telling Lorenzo that if he follows the guidelines set down in the preceding chapter, he should have no difficulty in conquering Italy, which, like France, is divided among many rulers. On the other hand, Lorenzo will not be able to rest on his laurels, for regional and local loyalties will remain and constantly crop up. Therefore, the Prince must wipe out all the regional lords and their families once he captures their states. Again, this is what Cesare Borgia did in central Italy and what King Louis failed to do.

CHAPTER V

This is the last chapter devoted to the problems of princes in dealing with subjugated areas. Machiavelli says that a state accustomed to liberty and its own laws can be retained only by one of three courses of action: the Prince must destroy it; or go and live there in person; or allow the people to live under their old laws, creating a government that will be friendly to the new Prince. Machiavelli seems to prefer the third alternative. Since the government of such a puppet state could not have come about were it not for the Prince's power, and would fall if that power were withdrawn, it would be loyal to him. "What is more, a city used to liberty can be more easily held by means of its citizens than in any other way, if you wish to preserve it."

Machiavelli illustrates this point by referring to the example of Sparta and the Romans. Sparta controlled Athens and Thebes through a government consisting of a few pro-Spartan individuals, and lost her conquests. The Romans utterly destroyed Capua, Carthage, and Numantia, and had no trouble holding them. After attempting the Spartan solution in Greece and finding it wanting, the Romans destroyed the cities of that area as well. This is the only true method of holding a people who are accustomed to freedom. "And whoever becomes the ruler of a free city and does not destroy it, can expect to be destroyed by it, for it can always find a motive for rebellion in the name of liberty and of its ancient usages." Such rebellions may be put off for many years, but are a constant danger. Pisa revolted against Florence after many years of control.

Such a problem will not exist in captured monarchies. There the people are used to leadership. All the new Prince has to do is kill the old one, and then wait for the people to select him as their new leader. "But in republics there is greater life, greater hatred, and more desire for vengeance. They do not and cannot cast aside the memory of their ancient liberty, so that the surest way is either to lay them waste or reside in them."

> **COMMENT:** Machiavelli warns Lorenzo not to deal with republics in the same manner as he would with monarchies. He realizes that the Prince cannot live physically in all the provinces he will capture while unifying Italy, so he recommends the only alternatives that seem possible. Lorenzo must either find collaborators within each city or destroy it; no other course is possible.

CHAPTER VI

It is well and good for the Prince to strike out on his own from time to time, but it is more sensible for him to follow the actions of his more successful predecessors. In this way, even if he is not completely successful, he will at least get some tinge of greatness. Machiavelli then repeats some of the lessons of earlier chapters, and concludes by saying that there are two methods by which a private individual can become a new Prince: either by good fortune or by great ability. Machiavelli says the Prince who has the former is better off, but here he will discuss those Princes who had great ability. The greatest of these were Moses, Cyrus, Romulus, and Theseus. With the possible exception of Moses, none of these leaders owed much to fortune. Rather, each was well qualified to take advantage of opportunities as they presented themselves.

Machiavelli then presents examples to support his contention that the right moment without the right man is wasted, and vice versa. Moses had to find the people of Israel slaves in Egypt; otherwise they would not have followed him. It was necessary for the ruler of Alba to expel Romulus; otherwise he would not have gone forth to found a great city. Cyrus had to find the Persians unhappy with the Medes, and the Medes weak, in order to gain control of the empire. Theseus could not have won victories if the Athenians had not dispersed before him. Thus, each man was presented by a golden opportunity, which he seized.

Princes such as these—who have ability but not necessarily good fortune—may have difficulties obtaining their states, but will not have difficulties retaining them. Their major problems revolve around the new laws and regulations they must formulate to secure their positions and establish the new state. This is a vital point to Machiavelli. "It must be considered that there is nothing more difficult to carry out, nor more doubtful of success, nor more dangerous to handle, than to initiate a new order of things." This is so because almost everyone in the state supports the old way of doing things, while few men actively seek change. People will not accept a new idea until they see it work; and how can they see it work unless they first accept it in part? For this reason, too, Machiavelli suggests that all armed prophets have succeeded, while the unarmed ones failed. Had any of his examples—Moses, Cyrus, Romulus, or Theseus—been disarmed at any point in his career, he would have failed. This is what happened to Savonarola. The monk believed completely in the new rules he gave to Florence, but did not bother to create an armed force to impel the people to accept them. Therefore, he was killed, and his reforms swept away. Then, there was the case of Hiero of Syracuse, who became Prince of his city when its inhabitants recognized his abilities and presented him with the post. Hiero abolished the old army and gave up his old friendships, and formed a new army and new alliances. With this firm foundation, he was able to rule Syracuse successfully.

COMMENT: In this chapter, Machiavelli faces a touchy problem. He wants Lorenzo to follow the example of Cesare Borgia, but can hardly put it in those terms. To do so, would be to imply that Lorenzo was less a prince than Cesare. Thus, the author resorts to classical examples in this chapter, and in the ones that follow. In addition, such references to classical figures were not unusual in the high Renaissance; Savon-

arola was hailed as a new Amos—a prophet bringing deliver-
ance to his people. So, Machiavelli implies, Lorenzo may
indeed be viewed as a new Moses, sent to bring the Italian
people out of foreign bondage and into the promised land
of national union.

CHAPTER VII

In Chapter VI, Machiavelli states that those who come to power
through great ability have difficulties in gaining power, but little
in maintaining it. The opposite is true of those who become princes
through good fortune: they take power easily, but find difficulties
in maintaining it. As examples, Machiavelli speaks of Princes who
are given states as favors, or who buy states for money. The former
will never be able to free themselves from the control of those who
gave them power, while the latter will always be insecure in command. In addition, such men are usually not of the type who know
how to command, and will suffer through errors and misjudgments.
Finally, such states, which usually develop quickly, have no time
to grow roots, and will be overwhelmed at the first opportunity.

To illustrate his points, Machiavelli discusses Francesco Sforza
and Cesare Borgia. Francesco gained control of Milan by virtue
of his abilities, and had little difficulty maintaining himself. On
the other hand, Cesare Borgia acquired his domain through his
father's influence, and when that influence was withdrawn, lost all.

Having introduced Cesare in this fashion, Machiavelli goes on to
analyze his rise and fall. He notes that Cesare's father, Pope Alexander VI, had difficulties finding a domain for his son. He knew
that it would be impossible to grant him Church land, because
such an action would bring swift opposition from Milan and other
states. The Pope further realized that the major military forces of
Italy were in the hands of those who would oppose such a move,
namely the Orsini and Colonna families. "It was, therefore, necessary to disturb the existing condition and bring about disorders in
the state of Italy in order to secure mastery over a part of them."
The question faced by Pope Alexander and his son, Cesare, was:
how to bring chaos to Italy, which could be used to their advantage?
The answer lay in the introduction of the French armies of King
Louis. Venice played into Cesare's hands by inviting French aid,
and the Pope cooperated by dissolving the King's marriage. As
soon as Louis arrived, the Pope obtained troops for him to use in
the taking of Romagna. Soon after, Cesare and Louis destroyed
the power of the Colonnas in Romagna, an action that was carried out with the aid of the Orsini family.

Now Cesare had a large domain, but he also had two major problems: (1) he doubted the loyalty of the Orsini family; (2) he
did not trust France. Cesare moved first against the Orsini, by
winning their followers in Rome. This was done through bribery

and promises of political favors. The Orsini learned of this, and called a meeting of their supporters at Magione. Rebellions followed, which were overcome by Cesare and the French armies.

Machiavelli also applauds Cesare, now a Duke, for his maneuverings in conquered lands. He writes that "having thus suppressed these leaders and their partisans, and having made their followers his friends, the Duke had laid a very good foundation for his power." The Duke did well in ruling Romagna, an area that had previously been controlled by weak men. He named Messer Remirro de Orco his governor there. A cruel and able man, he crushed all opposition in short order. Then the Duke, in order to appear kind and merciful, and gain the support of the people of Romagna, named a civil court of justice to investigate complaints against the governor. Within a little time, the people came to understand: (1) that the Duke was a harsh man, as witnessed by the governorship of de Orco; (2) that the Duke was a just man, as witnessed by the actions of his court against de Orco's excesses. This situation was not lacking in dangers: what if the people concluded that it meant the Duke did not completely control matters? This problem was resolved by killing de Orco in a bloody and dramatic fashion.

The Duke was now powerful and secure, and it only remained for him to gain the respect of France. For the time being, he bided his time, vacillating when France asked his aid in taking Milan from the Spanish armies. At this point too, Pope Alexander died, and was succeeded by forces hostile to the Borgias (Pope Julius II). Cesare now had to guard against those who would take his land from him. This was done in four ways: (1) he killed all those who might claim the crowns of the conquered lands; (2) he worked to win the friendship of Roman nobles who might act as a counterforce against the Pope; (3) he worked to gain the friendship of members of the College of Cardinals for the same reasons; (4) he tried to consolidate the power in Rome that he had acquired before the death of his father. The last three had been put into motion before the death of the Pope; now Cesare ordered all his opponents killed. Meanwhile, France and Spain had fought to a draw in Naples, and both states, now weakened, sought an alliance with Cesare. Thus emboldened, Cesare seized more and more land. Machiavelli implies that he could have taken all of Italy were it not for the untimely death of his powerful father.

The death of Alexander marked the beginning of the end for Cesare. Within a short time he was left with little but Romagna, pressed by opposing armies, and very ill physically. Even so, he held on, primarily because he had constructed the foundation of his power so well. Had it not been for his bad health, and the combined forces of his enemies, "he would have survived every difficulty." Further proof of his skill lay in the fact that when his enemies entered Rome, they could not find followers among the local leaders. Machiavelli writes that Cesare "told me on the day that Pope Julius II was elected, that he had thought of everything which might happen on the death of his father, and provided against everything, except that he had never thought that at his father's death, he would be dying himself."

Machiavelli reviews Cesare's career, and finds that he did little that was wrong. He could not and did not act incorrectly, "and his designs were only frustrated by the short life of Alexander and his own illness." Cesare's only mistake was not working harder to block the election of Pope Julius. Before becoming Pope, Julius had several grievances against Cesare; now that he had the power, he acted against the Borgias. Machiavelli writes that "men commit injuries either through fear or hate," and Julius both feared and hated Cesare. He thinks that Cesare would have been better served by the elevation of a Spanish Cardinal, who would have kept the difficulties with France alive.

> **COMMENT:** In this chapter, Machiavelli tries to show Lorenzo how Cesare operated, why he succeeded, and why he ultimately failed. Note that, according to Machiavelli, Cesare wins battles because of his skill, and loses in the end because of chance. This is not wholly true, for historically speaking, Cesare's difficulties with conquered provinces, except Romagna, were far greater than Machiavelli would have us believe. His problems began before the death of his father, and would have remained even if the Borgias had named one of their own to succeed Alexander.

CHAPTER VIII

There are two other ways of becoming a Prince: one may become a Prince through selection by his countrymen, or through villainy. Machiavelli will not go into detail on the first method, since this book does not deal with republics, but instead will dwell for a while on the second.

The author gives two examples by which a Prince gained power through villainy. Agathocles of Sicily became King of Syracuse after living most of his life as a poor man, the son of a potter. He was a most wicked man throughout. Agathocles was ambitious; he joined the militia and rose quickly to become praetor of Syracuse. At this point, he decided to become Prince, and "hold with violence and without the support of others that which had been constitutionally granted him." This ambition was told to Hamilcar the Carthaginian, who was fighting in Sicily at the time. Agathocles took power in a simple and brutal fashion. He called a meeting of all the important people and senators of Syracuse and, at a given signal, had them killed by his soldiers. Then he occupied the city with little difficulty. He defended the city successfully against Carthaginian attacks, although twice beaten in battle by Hamilcar.

Agathocles next invaded Africa, leaving a token force in the city. He was so successful there that the Carthaginians left Sicily to him, and were content to remain in Africa.

There are few aspects of Agathocles' career that can be interpreted as the results of good fortune. He worked his way up the ladder and, becoming Prince through murder and deceit, ruled with strength and determination. "It cannot be called virtue to kill one's fellow-citizens, betray one's friends, be without faith, without pity, and without religion; by these methods one may indeed gain power, but not glory." Machiavelli does not think less of Agathocles for his brutality or barbarism, but will not rank him among the great captains he has discussed in previous chapters. In a moment of somewhat strange morality (for him), Machiavelli states that "we cannot attribute to fortune or virtue that which he achieved without either."

In Machiavelli's own times, Oliverotto da Fermo was a prime example of how a Prince may gain power through villainy. A father-less boy, he was raised by an uncle and then sent as a soldier to Paolo Vitelli. When Paolo died, Oliverotto served under his brother, Vitellozzo, and soon became one of his captains. He then resolved to become a Prince in his own right. With the permission of Vitel-lozzo, he decided to conquer and rule Fermo.

Oliverotto then wrote a letter to his guardian, Giovanni Fogliani, in which he expressed a desire to visit him. In the letter, he mentioned that he would be accompanied by one hundred horsemen. Giovanni invited Oliverotto to Fermo, and lodged him and his followers in his houses. After waiting a few days, Oliverotto invited Giovanni and the leading citizens of Fermo to a great banquet. During the post-dinner discussions, Oliverotto spoke of Pope Alexander and Cesare Borgia, touchy topics for those days. After a few minutes of discussion, he suggested that such matters were best dealt with in a private place. Oliverotto led the men to a private room, where his soldiers were waiting. Within a short period of time, the guests were attacked, and all, including Giovanni Fogliani, were murdered. Then the soldiers rode to the home of the chief magistrate of Fermo, and forced him to accept the murderous Oliverotto as Prince. He named his friends to the positions left vacant through the murders, and within a year was the most feared and respected Prince in the region. He would have been as safe as Agathocles had it not been for his trust in Cesare Borgia, who killed him during his campaigns against the Orsini and Vitelli.

Machiavelli then asks how it is that men like Agathocles and Oliverotto can live secure in their states after years of treachery and deceit, while others are overthrown regularly. "I believe this arises from the cruelties being exploited well or badly." It is acceptable to use cruelty and deceit in order to gain power and to make it secure. Afterwards, however, the Prince should be circumspect in his actions. It is well to diminish, rather than increase, your cruelties as time goes on. If the population becomes used to and accepts barbaric treatment, the position of the Prince will not be secure.

"Whence it is to be noted, that in taking a state the conqueror must arrange to commit all his cruelties at once." The Prince who acts otherwise must always be ready for more conflict and murder. He can never depend upon his subjects, who have had wrongs inflicted upon them or expect such wrongs. "For injuries should be done all together, so that being less tasted, they will give less offence. Benefits should be granted little by little, so that they may be better enjoyed." Above all, the Prince must live among his subjects and be firm with them. In this way, the subjects will not rise against the Prince in bad times.

> COMMENT: Machiavelli does not expect Lorenzo to use the methods described in this chapter; to embark upon a career of villainy would bog down in local politics and leave little time for taking all of Italy. He demonstrates, however, how a Prince may be successful even if he lacks good fortune or ability, as described earlier. The lesson to be drawn from the examples of Oliverotto and Agathocles is this: the Prince must be ruthless if he is to succeed in taking power, but moderate once this power is achieved. Machiavelli will return to this theme on several occasions in the future.

CHAPTER IX

Machiavelli next turns to the situation that occurs when a Prince is chosen by his fellow citizens to become their leader. He discounts the possibility of having been chosen because of true worth or fortune, and instead demonstrates it is usually through "cunning assisted by fortune."

There are two factions in the state that may propel the Prince into power: the masses and the aristocracy; the Prince must obtain the support of one or the other. If the Prince would base his rule on the people, he must promise to oppress the nobility; the nobles will support him if he will oppress the people. There are three possible results from such a situation: rule by an oligarchy, by an individual, or by the people operating through a popular leader. If the nobles realize that the people will no longer accept their rule, they will place one of their number in power as Prince. Since the Prince is then only one among equals, he will find it difficult to rule without their support or concurrence, and an oligarchy will result. If the people believe the nobles are gaining too much power, they may place a Prince in power against the wishes of the nobles.

This Prince has far more power than the one previously described, for his supporters will not pretend to be on the same level as he.

Such a ruler will be able to act more fairly as well. To treat nobles with respect is to invite their scorn, while the masses react with gratitude to fair actions on the part of their rulers. This is so because "the aim of the people is more honest than that of the nobility, the latter desiring to oppress, and the former merely to avoid oppression." In addition, the Prince has less to fear if abandoned by the masses. They will merely desert him, while the nobles, once having withdrawn their support, tend to go into active opposition.

Machiavelli then expands upon the nature of those nobles who aid the Prince in obtaining power. He believes they must either be ruled or destroyed. The Prince must be careful in selecting those nobles to whom he gives trust and favors. They must be loyal, and be made to realize that their fortunes are tied to that of the Prince. Once they are found, they must be treated well, and given many rewards and promises of favors. As for those nobles who do not give support to the Prince, it must be realized that they either lack courage or ambition, or are in active opposition. The former may be won over; the latter are the greatest enemies the Prince has to face, and must be guarded against with great care.

A different set of problems and possibilities faces the Prince whose power is based on the masses. It will be relatively easy to retain mass support once it is granted; the people want little more than to be left alone. If the Prince has gained power without mass support, he should immediately try to win the backing of the people. This will not be difficult. When such a ruler comes into power, the people expect little of him. Any favors that he grants will be accepted gratefully, and they will soon consider him their benefactor. Machiavelli concludes by noting that it is vital for the Prince to have the support of the people, for "otherwise he has no resource in times of adversity."

As is his custom in the first part of The Prince, Machiavelli turns to classical history for examples that will illustrate his point. Nabis of Sparta was able to undergo a siege by all Greece and a Roman army and still maintain his position. When in danger, he trusted a few of his supporters, while at the same time assuring himself of mass support. Without the latter, the former would have been useless. Machiavelli discounts the old proverb, which states that "He who builds upon the people builds on mud." It is true that the Prince cannot rely upon the people to liberate him if he is captured or destroyed by his enemies. But it is also true that if the Prince has been wise, brave, and courageous, he will not be deceived by his people.

This is not to say that the people will be motivated out of love for the Prince. Rather, they will act only if convicted that they need him more than he needs them. Everyone is willing to defend the state in quiet times, when they feel they may need it for one reason or another. When the state is attacked and needs aid from the citizens, it will be deserted. Thus, the Prince must take care not to give too much power to magistrates, and rather rule as directly as possible. If the people see and know him, and think him responsible for their good fortune, they will support the Prince in his time of need as they would defend themselves.

> **COMMENT:** In the previous chapter, Machiavelli concentrated upon Princes who achieved power through treachery. Although he states that he will not discuss those who gain power through mass support, he feels it necessary to include a chapter on the subject. Machiavelli does not trust the masses; they are as fickle as nobles or rulers. But on occasions, they can and must be used for the Prince's ends. He makes distinctions between the actions and motivations of nobles and the people in this chapter, but although he does not say it directly, they have more in common than first meets the eye. Just as the nobles cannot be trusted unless their fortunes are tied to those of the Prince, so the people must be made to feel that the destruction of the Prince is their own destruction.
>
> Thus, nobles are untrustworthy in their way, and the people in another fashion. There is one major difference between them: the Prince may do away with those nobles who oppose him, but cannot destroy all of the masses who do not accept his rule. It is for this reason that he advocates the courting of the population. This is of special importance to Lorenzo, for in unifying Italy, he will need mass support, or else rely upon bands of ambitious nobles. To Machiavelli, the former is by far the more preferable.

CHAPTER X

In this chapter, Machiavelli develops some points made in the end of Chapter IX, where he discusses the problems of maintaining power in times of attack. In addition, he goes into the problems of allies, both internal and external.

The Prince must discover whether he needs the protection of others in defending the state. There is one test of this condition that must be made: the Prince must know whether he has enough men and money to form an army that can defend the state against all attackers. If he lacks these resources, and believes he must withdraw behind his walls and defend himself in time of attack, then he has need of allies. Should this be the case, the Prince must build his walls high for defense and ignore the rest of his domain. This is not to be done in order to give the impression of weakness. Rather, the enemy will be reluctant to attack lands belonging to a Prince whose town is well fortified, and whose people do not hate him.

Machiavelli cites the examples of the German cities to prove his point. They are free, have little to do with the countryside, and

do not feel oppressed by the Emperor. The cities are well fortified, and potential attackers do not consider their reduction,
which would take many years, to be worth the cost. The masses
are kept content by satisfying work, and are loyal to the state
since the work comes from that source. The German cities
conduct military exercises, and are in constant preparation for
any attack that might come.

The ruler of such a city cannot be assaulted. If any ruler would
be unwise enough to attack the city, he would be doomed to failure. A quick success would not be possible, since the town is well
defended. The attacker would then have to maintain a siege, and
would find it difficult to keep his armies idle while the tedious
job of destroying the defenses was completed. The attacker could
not hope to lower the people's morale by burning their homes and
laying waste to the countryside. The wise Prince, defending his
city, will tell his subjects that the siege cannot last forever. He
will enhance his power by turning the people's hatred against the
attacker. Thus, the longer and more severe the siege, the more
strength the wise Prince may gain. Further, after the attacker
leaves, the people will need the Prince's aid in rebuilding, and
in this way, draw still closer to him than before.

"It is the nature of men to be as much bound by the benefits that
they confer as by those they receive," is Machiavelli's conclusion.
It follows, then, that the wise Prince, who has prepared for
attacks, will be able to maintain control over the state.

COMMENT: To some commentators, this chapter seems out
of place. Previously, Machiavelli has discussed the various
types of states and how they should be ruled; in Chapter X,
he concentrates entirely upon the difficulties of siege opera-
tions. The reader must remember that Machiavelli is writing
this book for Lorenzo, both as a philosophical tract and, more
importantly, as a guide to action. He is not telling the Prince
in this case to concern himself with what to do if attacked;
rather, he is telling Lorenzo that if he plans to use military
force to capture the territories and cities of wise rivals, he
will be doomed to failure. Thus, he implies that such men
must be won over by other means.

CHAPTER XI

This is the last chapter of the first part of *The Prince,* and concludes Machiavelli's analysis of the different types of states, how
they may be obtained, and how they should be ruled. The author
discusses ecclesiastical principalities in this chapter, and in particular, the domain of the Catholic Church in Italy.

Church lands, says the author, are obtained by ability or fortune,
and retained by custom and tradition. By this, Machiavelli means

that the religious orders, like the secular princes, gain their
territories by force of arms or personality, or by other means used
by non-religious orders (see Chapter VI). Once obtained, however, different rules apply. So strong is the force of accepted religion that the Prince of an ecclesiastical state need do little to
maintain his power. These states are loyal without question;
"these princes alone have states without defending them, have
subjects without governing them, and their states, not being defended, are not taken from them; their subjects not being governed do not resent it, and neither think or are capable of aliena-
ting themselves from them." The author indicates that these
states are in a special category, and cannot be conquered by any
Prince, no matter how wise or fortunate he may be. He will discuss, however, how the Catholic Church managed to gain its
vast domain, especially since before the reign of Alexander VI
(1492-1503), it had little power in Italy. By referring in this
way to the great Borgia Pope, Machiavelli once more turns at-
tention to the methods by which the Prince may gain power. It
is for this reason that he feels justified in discussing the ecclesiastical states.

Before the French invasions of Italy, the country was ruled by
the Pope and the monarchs of Naples, Milan, and Florence. Each
of the Italian states feared both the French and their neighbors.
The two most powerful and ambitious Italian rulers were to be
found in Rome and Venice. The Venetians were checked by an
alliance of all the other Italian states, while the Pope was controlled by the Roman barons. This last group was divided into
the Orsini and Colonna factions, who were constantly quarreling
among themselves. This situation made it difficult for any Pope
to gain power. To overthrow the Colonna, he would need the aid
of the Orsini. This would place the Pope in the debt of the Orsini,
and at the same time lead to further struggles against the Colonna.

Because of this situation, the Pope was unable to exert his power.
But then Alexander VI was elected Pope and demonstrated how a
true Prince should behave in such a situation. He joined with
Cesare Borgia to expel the French. Cesare retained the lands
he conquered while alive, but on his death they were given to the
Church. When Pope Julius II became head of the Church in 1503,
he was most powerful. Romagna was his, and the Roman barons
had been suppressed. He was able to enlarge the Church's domains,
while at the same time keeping his rivals divided. The Pope was
able to accomplish this because the Church was widely respected
and feared, and because he had firm control over the cardinals. The
author makes a point of noting that men who occupy the position
of cardinals are the origin of many problems. They enter into
intrigues and draw the barons into Church affairs. Machiavelli
applauds both Julius II and his successor, Leo X, who "through
his goodness and infinite other virtues will make the Church both
great and venerated."

COMMENT: This last sentence, which is not characteristic of Machiavelli, was probably added because Leo X (1513-1521) was the son of Lorenzo the Magnificent and the uncle of Lorenzo de Medici, to whom *The Prince* was dedicated. In this chapter, Machiavelli indicates the great power of the Church, especially in Italy. He shows that a fortunate and talented Pope may gain power more easily than any other ruler. It is for this reason, among others, that Machiavelli will later condemn the Church for not taking the lead in the movement for the unification of Italy.

CHAPTER XII

In this chapter and the two that follow, Machiavelli deals with the means by which the Prince may defend himself against his enemies. In addition, through allusions and examples, he attempts to show Lorenzo why others have failed to conquer or unify Italy, how he may profit from their examples, and what guides he should use.

The most important assets of any state are good laws and good arms. These go together, for laws cannot operate unless backed by arms, and arms are useless without laws. The Prince may obtain arms from his people, or he may employ mercenaries—hired soldiers. Mercenaries are useless and dangerous; they cannot be trusted, are cowardly, and are faithless. The Prince who bases his rule upon such arms is in an insecure position. His mercenaries will not fight for him except for wages, and they will not risk their lives for money alone. Thus, they deplete the treasury in time of peace, and are almost useless in time of war. Machiavelli concludes that "the ruin of Italy is now caused by nothing else but through her having relied for many years on mercenary arms." Charles of France was able to conquer Italy for this reason. Had the Italian rulers used other than mercenary soldiers, he could never have succeeded. Machiavelli considers this point vital, and he returns to it on several occasions. Italy can never be united, he believes, unless there is a thoroughgoing reform of the armies.

With this in mind, Machiavelli launches into a detailed analysis of mercenary troops. Their leaders, if capable, cannot be trusted, for they will seek power on their own. If they are not capable, they will ruin the Prince through stupidities in the field. But do not all armies suffer from this problem? Machiavelli thinks not. All effective armies must be led by the Prince, or, in the case of a republic, its own citizens. If such a leader proves incompetent, he must be changed. Should he prove capable, his ambitions must be checked. These actions cannot be accomplished easily with mercenaries. The past has shown, says the author, that no nation which uses mercenaries has become great, and that such nations are more apt to surrender to opponents.

Machiavelli then launches into a series of historic examples. Rome and Sparta armed themselves and were free for many centuries. In his time, the Swiss, who did not employ mercenaries, were free and strong. On the other hand, the Carthaginians, who employed mercenaries, were oppressed by them. Philip of Macedon, who was a mercenary captain employed by Thebes, later deprived that city of its liberty. In recent history, Francesco Sforza turned against his Milanese employers after having defeated their Venetian enemies. Florence is the exception to the rule, and was not betrayed by its mercenaries. Machiavelli believes this was due to chance, for of those who might have attempted to overthrow the government, some were opposed by strong forces, others had their ambitions channeled elsewhere, and still others could not come to Florence with enough glory to attract supporters. For example, Sforza was checked by the Bracceshi, Francesco's ambitions were turned against Lombardy, and Sir John Hawkwood, who wanted to conquer Florence after having served as the city's mercenary, lacked military victories.

Next, Machiavelli turns to an affair of recent history, which would be familiar to Lorenzo. Florence appointed Paolo Vitelli, a man of the best reputation, as its commander. If Vitelli had conquered Pisa, as was hoped, Florence would have been in serious trouble. Vitelli's reputation, power, and following would have grown greatly. If he remained in Florence's service, he would have soon gained the power to control the city. Yet, even knowing this, the rulers of Florence could not let him go, for then he would have joined the enemies of the city and sooner or later destroyed it. A similar situation existed in Venice, which had many military victories while its armies were controlled by natives. Then one of Venice's generals, a mercenary named Carmagnola, gained an impressive victory over Milan. Venice, realizing it could no longer employ the ambitious Carmagnola, and could not afford to let him go over to the enemy, had him killed. He was replaced by less ambitious mercenary leaders, who were also less talented, and a series of failures resulted.

Why, then, do the Italian states employ mercenaries? Machiavelli believes that the troubles began after the Empire was repudiated in Italy. The Pope gained a great deal of power, at the expense of the once-powerful and self-sustaining states. These states then became the battleground between Pope and Emperor, and lost still more power and vigor. "Thus Italy, having fallen almost entirely into the hands of the Church and a few republics, and the priests and other citizens not being accustomed to bearing arms, they began to hire foreigners as soldiers." Alberigo da Como was the first to do this, and others soon followed. As a result of this, "Italy has been overrun by Charles, preyed upon by Louis, tyrannized over by Ferrando, and insulted by the Swiss."

Machiavelli is particularly angered by the Swiss, who discredited the infantry and restricted themselves to the cavalry because the latter force received more money and honors and, by implication, did less good for the state. Thus, the Swiss mercenaries, who were used by many Italian states, did little work and received most of the power and money. The risks in war were borne by the Italian infantrymen, while the Swiss cavalry refused to attack at night or undertake any dangerous assignments. Such foreigners have reduced Italy to slavery and degradation.

> **COMMENT:** As we have seen, Machiavelli objects to the Papacy for failing to unite Italy, and to foreigners who despoil his nation. The tone of this chapter is that of Machiavelli the fervent nationalist, but the content is still that of the practical man of affairs. If the author's sensibilities are hurt by mercenaries, his intelligence also tells him that they are not the best kind of troops to place in the field. Thus, he urges Lorenzo to rid his army of them. Since the Florentines had a long tradition of using Swiss mercenaries, his attack on them is particularly severe.

CHAPTER XIII

Machiavelli continues his discussion of military affairs by considering the nature of auxiliary troops. Such troops, which are borrowed from one's neighbor, are as useless as mercenaries. Auxiliaries may fight well, but they present dangers to the Prince who uses them, which are similar to those that exist when mercenaries are employed. If they lose, the Prince is defeated; if they win, he becomes their prisoner.

To illustrate his point, Machiavelli turns to the example of Pope Julius II, who was discussed in the previous chapter as well. His actions in gaining territory seemed most prudent. In his drive to conquer Ferrara, he was obliged to use foreign allies. If there had been only two forces in the field, the Pope would have suffered the evils of either a mercenary and auxiliary victory or defeat. As it was, a third force entered the field. Swiss soldiers rose up when the Pope's auxiliaries were defeated and drove back the victors. Because of this, the Pope was able to escape unscathed. The defeat of his auxiliaries prevented them from controlling him, and the defeat of his enemy prevented them from taking him captive.

If the Prince wants to assure failure, he may use auxiliaries. They can be as dangerous as mercenaries, who are at least disunited and owe allegiance to no one. Auxiliaries are united, and therefore can act together. In addition, they are controlled by someone other than the Prince. "In a word, the greatest danger with mercenaries lies in their cowardice and reluctance to fight, but with auxiliaries, the danger lies in their courage."

The Prince, if wise, would do best to avoid such soldiers altogether. It is better to lose with your own men than to win with troops

belonging to someone else. Machiavelli turns to the example of
Cesare Borgia, his hero, to illustrate this point. Cesare conquered
Romagna with auxiliaries, and captured Imola and Forli. But he
did not trust these troops, and after ridding himself of them, hired
the Orsini and Vitelli as mercenaries. He found these troops un-
faithful, suppressed them, and then relied upon his own men.
Machiavelli notes that Cesare's reputation was not high when he
used the auxiliaries, rose only slightly when he conquered with the
aid of mercenaries, and reached its height when he had victories
with his own men.

Hiero of Syracuse, an ancient leader, offers another example to
illustrate Machiavelli's point. Soon after being chosen as military
commander by his city, Hiero realized the uselessness of the mercenaries in the army. Thinking it unsafe either to keep them or let
them go, he had them killed. Then he entered into war at the head
of his own army, and had many victories. The story of King David,
in the Old Testament, offers still another example of the uselessness
and danger of mercenaries and auxiliaries. Machiavelli observes
that when David volunteered to fight Goliath, King Saul offered
him his own arms. David refused, and used his own instead. "In
short, the arms of others either fail, overburden, or else impede
you." Machiavelli might have added that in this instance, David
was acting as Saul's mercenary. Having gained a victory, he soon
took Saul's throne as well. Thus, even in victory, the Prince suffers
defeat when mercenaries are used.

Charles VII of France was able to liberate France from England,
and he too recognized the wisdom of using one's own men. His
successor, King Louis XI, soon abolished the French infantry and
hired Swiss soldiers instead. This was a grave mistake. The Swiss
mercenaries have gained a great reputation, which has disheart-
ened those French troops loyal to the King. Now the French soldiers believe they cannot win victories without the aid of the
Swiss, and they will not fight without them. Thus, the French
armies are in the hands of the Swiss mercenaries. France employs
a mixed army, made up of mercenaries and loyal troops. This is
better than having a force comprised solely of mercenaries or
auxiliaries, but it is not as good as an army of loyal men. France
would have been invincible if Charles' army was retained intact.
As it is, that nation has several weaknesses. The French rulers do
not realize this; they are not wise. Yet, few are granted wisdom.
Even the Romans were blind to this problem. The Empire began
to fall when the emperors began hiring Goth mercenaries. Within
a short time, the Goths controlled the Empire.

Machiavelli concludes by repeating that no prince may be secure
without his own troops. If one does not heed this warning, he will
have to depend solely upon fortune for success.

COMMENT: In Chapters 12, 13, and 14, the author is concerned with the military methods by which the Prince may gain and consolidate his power. He begins with the worst case, that of using mercenaries. In this chapter, he discusses auxiliaries, which are only slightly better. The pattern of discussion indicates that in the following chapter, he will analyze the correct type of army for the wise Prince. Thus, this entire section may be viewed as an argument from the worst to the best of situations. In this case, Chapter 13 may be viewed as transitional.

CHAPTER XIV

How may the Prince be successful in his endeavors? By studying little but war, for that is the only art necessary for one who commands. Correct knowledge of war can keep a Prince who has been born to rule in power, and may enable those who were not born princes to rise to that position. When princes think of other matters, and neglect the arts of war, they will lose their domains. "The chief cause of the loss of states is the contempt of war, and the way to acquire them is to be well versed in the same."

Francesco Sforza, a private citizen, learned the arts of war, and through their use became Duke of Milan. His sons, who were not interested in war, lost Milan and became private citizens. The Prince who is uninterested in war becomes contemptible, and this attitude on the part of others must be guarded against at all costs. This should be obvious. An unarmed man is obliged to obey one who has arms, and an unarmed man cannot be considered safe if his servants have arms. So it is that the Prince, if ignorant of war and unarmed, is not regarded with respect by his soldiers and so cannot have confidence in them.

The Prince must study the arts of war at all times. He must do this by actions and by learning from the experiences of others. His army must be kept disciplined and on guard. The Prince must study the nature of his terrain, and must formulate plans of attack and defense. Such knowledge will always be useful. It will enable 'the Prince to know his country better, and so better defend it. In addition, the practice gained in such study will benefit the Prince when he attacks his enemies. For example, if the Prince studies and then formulates plans regarding the attack of a hill in his domain, he will be able to use this experience in attacks on other hills. The Prince who lacks this skill lacks the first essentials of leadership. It is this sort of planning that enables the Prince to find his enemy, organize his forces for the attack, lead armies, plan battles, and lay siege to fortifications.

Philopoemen, a Prince of Achaei, was often praised because it was thought that in times of peace, he did not think of war. But was this really so? Often while walking with friends, he would stop to look at a hill, then ask and discuss questions of attack and defense regarding it. Philopoemen was continually thinking of war, and so was never caught off guard when war came.

The Prince should also study history, and reflect on the actions of famous and great men. How did such men gain victories? What mistakes did they make? Machiavelli indicates that one may learn from the past, and may follow great men when correct, and avoid their errors. This has always been so, for the great men of the past did themselves study other models. Alexander the Great imitated Achilles, and Caesar imitated Alexander. The wise Prince will imitate these and other models. He will never rest, and will continually try to better himself.

> COMMENT: Having made his major point—that the Prince must rely upon his own men for support—Machiavelli adds that once his men enable the Prince to gain power, he must take care not to lose it. One cannot know what Machiavelli was referring to here, if indeed he wanted to tell Lorenzo anything at all. However, it should be noted that Savonarola, having captured Florence, ignored military studies to turn to a religious reformation. One might say that Machiavelli was warning the present ruler of Florence, Lorenzo de Medici, to avoid the mistakes made by the earlier ruler of the city. If this is so, then the last section of the chapter, in which Machiavelli suggests that the Prince would do well to study history, takes on added meaning.

CHAPTER XV

In this chapter, and the eight that follow, the author discusses the attributes and actions of a Prince in power. Many scholars believe that this is the heart of the book, and presents the most deeply felt thoughts the author had regarding the nature of leadership and its rewards. In this section, Machiavelli attacks previous writers on the subject and attempts to formulate his own philosophy of leadership.

Machiavelli makes his intent in this regard quite clear from the outset. He notes that many other writers have discussed these questions, and he hopes the reader will not judge him presumptuous for differing with them on many points. He intends to write on real problems, rather than abstractions—"to go to the truth of the matter rather than to its imagination"—and present a practical guide for the Prince. The way we live is far removed from the way we should live, and Machiavelli is more interested in the former than the latter. If a man tries to do the right thing in all he does, he will come to grief, for none of his companions and enemies are that good themselves. "Therefore it is necessary for a Prince, who wishes to maintain himself, to learn how not to be good, and to use this knowledge and not use it, according to the necessity of the case."

All princes are blamed or praised for imaginary qualities. One may be considered miserly, while another is thought of as liberal; this prince has the reputation of being merciful, while that one is spoken of as cruel. It is considered good to be thought of as having fine, noble qualities, even though no ruler can really be as fine as his more ardent followers think him to be. Yet, the Prince should try to have the reputation of excellence in all he is and does, even if this is not true. In other words, he should take care that his subjects think him kind, trustworthy, frank, chaste, honest, etc. But what if the exercise of some of these qualities would lead to the Prince's ruin, as Machiavelli thinks they would? In that case, the Prince should not hesitate to take whatever actions necessary, however ignoble, in order to further his interests.

COMMENT: Machiavelli is walking on thin ice in this short, introductory chapter. In effect, he is suggesting that the Prince neither know nor recognize any authority other than that of power and expediency. This is a difficult suggestion, written as it was during the height of Church power and to a Prince whose uncle was the Pope. On more careful examination, however, it becomes clear that what Machiavelli is suggesting is not as radical as might seem at first blush. The Renaissance Church was corrupt, and anyone in a position of power, including Lorenzo, must have known this. Such a person would also realize that in the world of Renaissance Italy, certain actions were necessary in politics that did not comply with the public morality of the Church, and that the Church itself was perhaps the greatest transgressor of its own teachings. Machiavelli indicates that if the Church leaders, especially the Renaissance Popes, had acted in accord with Christian ethics, they could never have amassed the territories they controlled. Thus, if Lorenzo would gain power, he must appear to be all good to his followers, but prepare to take any action needed to gain his ends.

CHAPTER XVI

Machiavelli now develops the point made in the previous chapter. It is well to be considered liberal, but if you are truly liberal, you may be easily injured. The truly liberal man does his work without fanfare and does not advertise his good works. What good would it do the Prince to be truly liberal, if this is the case? In point of fact, the truly liberal Prince runs the danger of being considered illiberal. If the Prince desires the reputation of being liberal, he must be very showy and ostentatious. He must live beyond his means and, if necessary, impose heavy taxes on his subjects. This will lead to opposition on the part of the people, and the slightest disturbance in the state will be magnified into grave threats to his power. If the would-be liberal Prince then attempts to change his ways, and cuts expenses and favors, he will be thought of as being miserly, which the people consider

a vice. Thus, Machiavelli concludes, the Prince should not attempt to be thought of as being liberal, or free with his and other
people's assets.

The Prince, then, should not object to being considered miserly
In time, the people will recognize that his refusal to spend funds
wildly and, by necessity, tax them, is true liberality. If he does
this, his revenue will be more than enough to provide him with
arms for defense and attack. If war does come, his people will
appreciate not being taxed for its support. In such a way, he will
increase his power. Those who will not be taxed are many, while
those who will not receive grants are few. *Should be cheap*

Machiavelli notes that those rulers who attempted to gain the
reputation of being liberal have suffered, while those who were
reputed to be miserly have prospered. Pope Julius II sought the
reputation of liberality in order to gain the Papacy. He indicated
to supporters his willingness to reward them, and actually did
so in many cases. Once he attained the Papacy, all was changed.
If he had continued to make large grants to his supporters, he
would have lacked funds to conduct his many wars. Similarly,
the French King has been able to conduct wars because he prac-
tices economies at home, and the King of Spain also follows this
pattern.

For these reasons, the Prince should not mind being thought of
as miserly. Only in this way can he retain power. It is true
that Caesar and others gained power through liberality and
large grants. Machiavelli replies that such actions are acceptable
only when power is desired, and never when power is actually
possessed. Caesar had to grant gifts while seeking control of the
Empire; had he not acted in such a way, his followers would
have left him. On the other hand, had he continued to act with
liberality after gaining power, he would have destroyed the Empire. He adds that if money has to be spent, the Prince is faced
with the choice of using his own funds, those of his subjects, or
those of others. He should never spend his own money, but may
spend as much of other people's money as is necessary to gain
power. This is particularly true for the Prince who marches with
his army, which will not fight unless it may plunder and gain
booty.

Caesar, Cyrus, and Alexander, the great conquerors of ancient
times, acted in such a fashion. Spending the wealth of others
serves to increase the Prince's reputation; spending his own
money injures his position. "There is nothing which destroys itself
so much as liberality, for by using it you lose the power of
using it, and become either poor and despicable, or, to escape pov-
erty, rapacious and hated." It is of great importance for the Prince
not to be despised or hated, and that is where liberality will lead
the unwise Prince who adopts it as his policy. The reputation

of miserliness produces disgrace; the reputation of rapaciousness, which comes from liberality, produces both disgrace and hatred.

COMMENT: Machiavelli wrote *The Prince* in the world of Renaissance Italy, in a time and place noted for its splendor and extravagance. He was writing for Lorenzo de Medici of Florence, the intellectual center of the Renaissance. Lorenzo's grandfather, Lorenzo the Magnificent, was one of the greatest patrons of the arts the world had ever known. It is for these reasons that Machiavelli stresses the importance of frugality. If Lorenzo attempts to emulate his fellow monarchs, he will never be a great ruler of men. This will be a difficult choice to make, for should Lorenzo withdraw funds from the artists and writers of Florence, he will lose their support and go contrary to the traditions of the city. Machiavelli seems to brush this kind of criticism aside. He is interested in political and military power, and not in artistic reputation.

Machiavelli doesn't give a shit about Renaissance ⟶ POWER

CHAPTER XVII

Just as the Prince may desire to appear liberal, but must not be liberal, so he may desire to be considered merciful, but must "take care not to misuse this mercifulness." Cesare Borgia, who was considered cruel, nonetheless brought order to Romagna and then controlled it. This is, in actuality, the essence of true mercy. By acting in a cruel fashion, Cesare prevented Romagna from falling into unwise hands and being destroyed. This was far more merciful than the acts of the Florentines who, in attempting to avoid cruelty, allowed the city of Pistoia to be destroyed by others. Therefore, the Prince should not mind being considered cruel, if his purpose in acting is to keep his subjects united and faithful. The tender-hearted, through their misguided softness, allow insurrections to develop, which do more harm than the harshest Prince. The Prince should also realize that it is almost impossible for any new ruler to escape the reputation of being cruel, for he must act swiftly to establish control over the state, and such acts are usually considered unfair. The Prince should not fear such a reputation, for it is necessary.

Machiavelli then turns to a related question: "Is it better to be loved or feared?" It is best to be both loved and feared, he replies, but should this prove impossible, the wise Prince will choose to be feared. This is so because of the nature of mankind. The author then develops his ideas as to human nature. Men in general, he says, are ungrateful, eager to avoid danger, and selfish. They should never be trusted, for, the moment you need them, they will flee. If man is indeed this way, how can one appeal to his nobler side (since it doesn't exist) or ask him to act against self-interest (since that is the only interest he recognizes)? Mankind in general lacks the qualities that make some

The BIG question

Bronx Tale

individuals respond to love. They have little respect for people who make this appeal to them. "Love is held by a chain of obligation which, men being selfish, is broken whenever it serves their purpose." On the other hand, "fear is maintained by a dread of punishment which never fails."

Be this as it may, the Prince must take care not to be feared so much that he is hated. If the Prince does not take his subjects' women or property, their hatred will not be earned. If a subject must be killed, let it be done for good and sufficient reason. This is not as important, however, as refraining from the taking of property. One may forgive the murder of one's father, but one never forgets the seizure of property. So, if property must be taken, let the Prince do so for excellent reasons. These are never hard to find.

A different situation exists when the Prince marches at the head of his army. Then he should not mind being thought of as cruel. Indeed, it may be necessary to have this reputation, for this is what keeps an army together. It was in this way that Hannibal kept his diverse armies together. If Hannibal had not been so cruel, he could not have gained the support of his men. "Thoughtless writers admire on the one hand his actions, and on the other blame the principal cause of them."

The case of Scipio further illustrates this point. Because of his kindness, his armies revolted, and Scipio was denounced as a corrupter of the Roman militia. Were Scipio living under the Empire, which Machiavelli admired, instead of the Republic, which he thought weak and ineffectual, his kindness would have been thought a flaw instead of a virtue.

Machiavelli concludes by noting that men love freely, but fear at the will of the Prince. The wise Prince may better exercise his power in this fashion.

COMMENT: Machiavelli was interested in stripping away the world of pretense and looking at what he considered reality. Before this could be done, he must formulate a theory of human conduct based not upon the Christian ethic, as other writers had done before him, but rather upon what he considered observable phenomena. This chapter is significant because in it Machiavelli spells out his view of the nature of man, a view he returns to on several other occasions and which may be found in all his writings. Once this view is accepted, he believes, all else will flow logically into order.

CHAPTER XVIII

In this chapter, Machiavelli discusses the ways by which the Prince may keep good faith, and the conditions under which good faith must be abandoned. This analysis must be viewed against the background of the previous chapter, in which the author sets forth his view of mankind. Like the rest of the chapters in this section, it deals first with what the Prince will desire insofar as appearances are concerned, and then what he must do in order to gain power and retain it.

Machiavelli begins by conceding that all know that it is good for the Prince to keep his word and preserve his integrity. Still, history shows that many princes who did not keep their words, and who engaged in double dealings, were quite successful. Such Princes often overcome those who are admired.

There are two methods of fighting: by law or by force. Men fight by laws, while beasts use force. But if the first method does not result in victory, should not man use the second? Therefore, the wise Prince will learn both methods and use them. Machiavelli finds an example of this in the story of Achilles, who was supposed to have been raised by Chiron, the centaur. This is one of the poorest examples to be found in the book, but it is followed by what is probably the most often quoted paragraph in *The Prince*:

"A prince who must act as a beast must imitate the fox and the lion. For the lion cannot protect himself from traps and the fox cannot defend himself from wolves. One must therefore be a fox to recognize traps and a lion to frighten wolves. Those who wish to be only lions do not understand this. Therefore, a prudent ruler ought not to keep faith when by doing so it would be against his interest, and the reasons which made him bind himself no longer exist."

The meaning of this paragraph is quite clear: the Prince must be as strong as the lion when such strength is called for, and as cunning as the fox, when need be. In other words, Machiavelli calls upon the Prince to use his power ruthlessly, and not to concern himself too much with questions of good faith and conscience. If all men were good, such actions would not be necessary. This is not the case. Since men are bad, and would not keep their word to you, you need not worry unduly about breaking your word to them. If necessary, the wise Prince can find many reasons to justify the breaking of a trust. Machiavelli offers countless examples of this. The Prince must act as a fox and be a great falsifier. He need not concern himself too much about the chances of his being discovered. Men are fools, and the Prince who deceives will always find people who allow themselves to be deceived. Machiavelli then notes that Pope Alexander VI "did nothing else but deceive men, he thought of nothing else." No man ever gave his word more often or in greater solemnity, and no man broke his word on as many occasions.

Machiavelli then concludes that it is not necessary for the Prince to be merciful, humane, kind, and faithful, although it may be

necessary to appear to have these qualities. He notes that it may
be dangerous for the Prince to possess these qualities, for they
tend to limit his range of actions. This is especially true of new
princes, for in order to solidify their power, they must act ruthlessly against any and all opponents. Perhaps with tongue in
cheek, he ends the paragraph by saying that the Prince should
be good unless and until he must do evil, and implies that it is
always necessary to do evil.

As for his subjects, the Prince should appear to possess all the virtues. Men will see the surface of your actions, and not understand
or care to understand what lies below them. "Everybody sees
what you appear to be, few feel what you are, and those few
will not dare to oppose themselves to the many, who have the
majesty of the state to defend them." In the actions of men, especially princes, the end justifies the means. If the Prince is
successful in gaining and maintaining power, his means will be
considered honorable, and will be praised by all. The vulgar
(stupid) people are only interested in appearances, "and the
world consists only of the vuglar." Machiavelli says that he knows
of one Prince who speaks of nothing but peace and good faith,
but is warlike and continually breaks his word. Had he acted
according to what he said, he would have lost his position long
ago. Many commentators believe that Machiavelli is referring
here to the Pope. *Ranking on the clergy*

> **COMMENT:** To many, this is the most important chapter
> in *The Prince*. In it Machiavelli makes his most pungent
> comments on human nature, and makes his boldest suggestions
> as to the actions of the Prince. In any case, Chapter XVIII is
> certainly the most quoted chapter of the book, and the one
> referred to when the term "Machiavellian" is used. There
> is no doubt that this represented the essence of the author's
> thoughts. He hardly bothers to refer to the ancients for ex-
> amples, as he does on other occasions when he feels he is
> skating on thin ice. He ends with an attack on a reigning
> ruler, which is hardly the action of a prudent man.

CHAPTER XIX

This is the longest chapter of *The Prince*, and in many ways the
most learned. Machiavelli, having dropped his bombshell in the
preceding chapter, attempts here to amplify his statements and
buttress them with solid arguments. The title of Chapter XIX is
"That We Must Avoid Being Despised and Hated," but in actuality it deals with a much larger range of problems the Prince must
face.

If the Prince avoids those actions that will make him hated or
despised, he will find little danger in other mistakes or vices he
may encounter. The author then all but repeats the argument of
Chapter XVIII, as though to underline the important points made

in that section. The Prince must be firm, he says. Such a show of strength will discourage his enemies and gain him adherents.

Such a Prince will soon have a great reputation, and it is difficult to engage in conspiracies against such a ruler. The respected Prince will have few difficulties, since all princes have only two fears: those involving their subjects and those involving potential foreign enemies. He can deal with foreign enemies if he has good soldiers and good arms, and a strong and wise Prince will always have these. Internal matters will remain stable, since they will not be disturbed by foreign agitation or internal conspiracy against the strong Prince. In any event, the strong Prince will be able to deal with whatever problems may arise. If the Prince avoids being hated and despised, internal intrigues will not develop. One of the best ways to avoid conspiracies is to be loved by the mass of the people. "For whoever conspires always believes that he will satisfy the people by the death of their Prince." If the potential conspirator knows that the Prince is popular, he will not attempt to organize plots against his life and power.

It is difficult to mount a successful conspiracy, and history shows that few plots are successful. Conspirators cannot act alone; they must have companions. These companions are to be found among the malcontents of society. If they are brought into a plot, they will soon realize that they can satisfy all their needs by betraying their companions to the Prince and in this way cease being malcontents. Thus, the only people in the state who might join in a conspiracy are the very ones who would most easily betray it. The plotters will have to be most careful in choosing their companions. These will be the people who have violent hatred for the Prince or are close friends of the leader of the conspiracy. But the former are frightened by the chance of failure, while the latter are awed by the majesty of the Prince. The author then concludes that "it is impossible that any one should have the temerity to conspire." If the Prince is popular, and the conspiracy succeeds in overthrowing him, the people will rise up and destroy the conspirators. If it fails, they will be killed by the Prince.

There are many examples of unsuccessful conspiracies against strong princes, and Machiavelli chooses one that occurred in the recent past. The Prince of Bologna, Annibale Bentivogli, was assassinated by the Canneschi. Although he left no relations save an infant son, the people of Bologna rose up and killed all the Canneschi. This was done because the Bentivogli had earned the goodwill of the people. Indeed, so great was this goodwill that the people of the city invited a member of the family who lived in Florence and was thought to be the son of a blacksmith to come to Bologna and rule until the infant Giovanni was old enough to assume power.

Machiavelli concludes that the ruler of a state in which the people are happy has little to fear from conspiracies, while those who rule

states in which the population hates those in power must fear
everything and everyone. Therefore, the Prince should attempt to
satisfy his people.

Machiavelli considers France to be well ordered and governed.
That nation has many good institutions that depend on the King,
among which the most important is the estates general. This body,
which contains representatives of the people, acts as a check on
the ambitions of the nobles. Further, the power of the nobles acts
to check the potential ambitions of the estates general. In this way,
the King rules without fear, for each group courts his support
against the other. Unpopular actions are left to be carried out by
one or the other of these two groups. Machiavelli feels that the
Prince should never be responsible for the issuance of unpopular
decrees, and so applauds the French system. He concludes by
saying that the Prince should hold his nobles in esteem and not
make himself hated by the general population.

Machiavelli feels that some of his critics might think the successful depositions of many Roman emperors demonstrate the falsity
of his claims. Some of these rulers lived good lives, enjoyed the
support of the population, and yet were overthrown by conspiracies. The author then launches into a discussion of Roman history
to prove this contention false, which he will do by examining
Roman leaders from Marcus Aurelius to the first Maximinus.
Before discussing each of these emperors individually, he notes
that whereas other rulers have to deal only with the ambitions of
the nobles and the insolence of the population, the Roman emperors had to concern themselves with the cruelty and ambitions
of the army as well. Since it is almost impossible to please both
the population and the army at the same time, many emperors
failed through the opposition of one or the other. The people prefer peace, while soldiers desire war. No prince can satisfy both
demands at the same time.

Emperors who lacked military reputations and kept the peace, or
who had such reputations and went to war, were doomed to
failure. Since most of the emperors of this period were "new
men," they concentrated on satisfying the soldiers, and tended
to ignore the people. This choice was necessary, but unfor-
tunate. Still, the emperors should have made a greater effort
to gain the support of the people. If this could not have been
done, then they should have tried to escape the hatred of the most
powerful groups in the population. The emperors who failed were
unable to accomplish this. So it was that Marcus Aurelius, Pertinax, and Alexander, all of whom were excellent men, came to sad
ends. Marcus alone was able to die in honor, and then only because he had succeeded to the position of emperor by hereditary
rights, and did not owe his position to either the soldiers or the
people. In addition, he was never hated or despised. On the other
hand, Pertinax became emperor against the will of the army, and,
because he attempted to reform the army, he failed.

From this Machiavelli concludes that "hatred is gained as much by good works as by evil." Therefore, the Prince may as well do evil if need be to accomplish his ends. This is especially true if your opponent is corrupt; in that case, good works often do more harm than good. The author then cites the case of Alexander, who was considered one of the kindest and most just of the Roman emperors. Nevertheless, because it was felt that he was ruled by his mother and was effeminate, Alexander was opposed by the army. Leaders of the army conspired against him, and Alexander was assassinated.

Consider, on the other hand, the qualities of men like Commodus, Severus, Antoninus, Caracalla, and Maximinus. These were cruel and unjust men who, in attempting to gain the support of the soldiers, inflicted many evils on the people. All ended badly except Severus. He was able to maintain himself in power, despite his oppression of the people. The soldiers respected him and were content under his rule, while the people were astonished and stupefied by his oppressions. Although Machiavelli does not mention it, Severus died at the sword of his enemies, after his army deserted.

At this point, Machiavelli returns to his examples of the lion and the fox, which he applies to the life of Severus. This leader realized that Emperor Julianus was lazy, and that the opportunity existed for him to seize control of the Empire. He persuaded his army to go with him to Rome to avenge the murder of Pertinax, who had been killed by the Praetorian Guard, when actually he planned to kill the Emperor while at the head of his troops. He quickly marched to Rome, catching the city by surprise. The senate elected him Emperor through fear of his power and then killed Julianus.

Then Severus faced his major problems. Nigrinus, who commanded the Asian armies, had proclaimed himself emperor, while Albinus, whose command was in the West, showed signs of great ambition. Severus knew it would be dangerous to fight both men at the same time, so he decided to first attack Nigrinus while deceiving Albinus. He wrote Albinus, telling him that he wished to share the imperial office with him, and sending him the title of Caesar. Then the senate named Albinus the colleague of Severus. With Albinus out of the way, Severus marched eastward, defeated and killed Nigrinus, and placed his supporters in positions of command in that part of the Empire. He then returned to Rome, where he charged Albinus with having conspired to assassinate him. Because of this, he said, Albinus would have to be destroyed. Severus then marched to France, where he met and killed his last rival.

Machiavelli considers Severus to have been both a ferocious lion and an astute and clever fox. He was feared and respected by all, and was not hated by the army. His great reputation defended him against the hatred his greed might have produced in the people. His son, Antoninus, also a man of great ability, possessed qualities similar to those of Severus. But his ferocity and cruelty were so great—he killed a large part of the populations of Rome and Alexandria—that he was universally hated. Antoninus began to fear assassination plots, and indeed was finally killed by an officer in his army. At this point, Machiavelli reflects on the nature of such assassinations. He notes that "this kind of death, which proceeds from the deliberate action of a determined man, cannot be avoided by princes, since any one who does not fear death himself can inflict it. But a prince need not fear much on this account, as such men are extremely rare." Instead, he should take care not to injure anyone he has need of, or has about him. This was the error of Antoninus. He had caused the death of the centurion's brother and was assassinated in revenge.

The author next turns to Commodus, the son of Marcus. This Emperor might easily have retained control of the Empire, for he succeeded his father. If he had followed Marcus' programs, and done little else, his reign would have ended happily. But Commodus was cruel and bestial. He granted many favors to the soldiers in order to gain their support of his persecutions of the people. He did not maintain his dignity, and often went into the arena to fight with the gladiators. These and other actions unworthy of an emperor soon won Commodus the contempt of the soldiers, and "being hated on the one hand and despised on the other, he was conspired against and killed."

Next, Machiavelli turns to Maximinus, an extremely warlike man who was elected emperor after the death of the effeminate Alexander. Maximinus lasted only two years, because he had two fatal flaws: he was a peasant, which made him despised, and he put off going to Rome to take possession of the imperial seat. Maximinus was also cruel and this, together with his base blood and flaunting of traditions, led to his downfall. At first he was conspired against in Africa, then by the senate, and finally by the people of Rome and all of Italy. His own army joined in the conspiracy. Seeing that Maximinus had so many enemies, and that they would not be punished for the crime, they put him to death.

Machiavelli will not discuss Heliogabalus, Macrinus, or Julianus, whom he considers contemptible. He notes, however, that the princes of his time have less difficulties with their armies than did the Romans. This is because the armies of the Renaissance are less concerned with political matters than those of ancient Rome. If it was necessary in Roman times to please the army more, it was because the army could do more for the Prince. Now, it is more necessary for the Prince to satisfy the people than the soldiers, for they can do more for the Prince. Machiavelli makes an exception of the Turks, for the large army of that empire is the basis for its power and security. A similar situation exists in the case of the Sultan, who is controlled by his soldiers.

In his concluding paragraph, Machiavelli states that whoever studies the arguments put forth in this chapter will easily see that hatred or contempt was the cause of the rulers' downfall. All made mistakes. Since Alexander and Pertinax were new rulers, they need not have attempted to imitate Marcus, who was a hereditary ruler. Similarly, Caracalla, Commodus, and Maximinus were wrong in attempting to imitate Severus, for they lacked his ability. A new Prince cannot imitate either Marcus or Severus, "but he must take from Severus those things that are necessary to found his state and from Marcus those that are useful and glorious for conserving a state that is already established and secure."

COMMENT: This chapter may be viewed as an elaboration of the previous chapter and a prelude for the next. In most of his chapters, Machiavelli concentrates on setting forth a broad statement, then offers one, or at most two examples to back up his contention. This chapter is the exception. No new ideas are presented, but Machiavelli concentrates on giving examples to support his contention that the Prince must avoid being despised and hated. There are probably several reasons for this. In the first place, since this is the major theme of the second part of *The Prince*, it would deserve a major statement. Then too, the writers of the Renaissance prided themselves on their classical erudition, and Machiavelli was no exception. Finally, some scholars believe that Machiavelli was not really talking about Roman emperors, but rather was presenting disguised accounts and analyses of contemporary figures, which would be recognizable to Lorenzo and others of his court.

CHAPTER XX

In the previous chapter, the author dwelt on the problems of new princes in gaining and maintaining their power. Through the use of examples from Rome, he shows that their difficulties are not the same as those of princes who rule through heredity. In this chapter, he generalizes more than in the previous one, and offers some conclusions based on information discussed earlier.

Princes use different means to retain and control their domains. Some disarm their citizens, others construct fortresses, and still others have destroyed fortresses. Each case must be considered on its own merits, but Machiavelli will attempt to make a few generalizations.

A new Prince has never disarmed his subjects. Instead, he has often given them arms with which to fight for his cause. In this way, the Prince's subjects become his partisans. All subjects cannot be armed, and those who receive arms will recognize the importance and honor of the distinction, and support the Prince all the more. Further, the Prince will be able to deal more effectively with the rest, since they lack power. When the Prince attempts to disarm his supporters, he runs into trouble. This will offend them, and show that they are distrusted because of their lack of fighting ability or the Prince's lack of confidence in their loyalty. Both of these opinions can easily lead to hatred, which must be avoided. Since the Prince cannot remain unarmed, he must resort to the use of mercenaries, which, as we have seen, are worse than useless. For this reason, the new Prince will always have his subjects armed.

When the ruler of a state adds another state to his domain, he must disarm the citizens of the new state, except those who aided in its capture. Even they must be weakened. All arms must be in the hands of soldiers from the old state. There is an old saying, "It is necessary to hold Pistoia by means of factions and Pisa with fortresses." Because of this, invaders fomented insurrections in some of the subject states, and in this way, possessed them more easily. This was well and good in the old days, but it does not seem wise for the present. When the enemy attacks, such divided cities always fall, for the weaker faction will side with the enemy and the stronger one will not be able to withstand the attack.

The Venetians followed the old rule and fomented conflicts between the Guelph and Ghibelline factions in the cities they conquered. In this way, the citizens were involved in their own quarrels, and did not unite against Venice. This did not benefit the Venetians, for after the defeat of Vailà, a part of the captive citizenry revolted and seized the state. In addition, the presence of open feuding indicates that the Prince is weak, for if he were strong, such outbreaks would not be possible. Such insurrections may be profitable in time of peace, when the Prince can control them, but they are most dangerous in time of war.

Princes become great when they overcome difficulties and opposition. Therefore, the fortunate Prince will have many enemies who want to seize his lands. In his victories over them, he will enhance his reputation and increase his stature. Indeed, some observers believe that the Prince should encourage his enemies to attack him for this very purpose.

Many princes, especially new ones, may find that they have greater use of men who they suspect of opposition than of those who are trusted. This is especially true at the beginning of the Prince's reign. Pandolfo Petrucci, Prince of Siena, governed in this fashion. The author says that enemies who need the Prince's support in order to retain their positions can be easily won over. They will work harder and be more loyal than the Prince's old friends, for they know that they must do well in order to cancel the bad opinion the Prince has of them. The Prince's friends, being secure in his trust, will not work as hard.

The new Prince must also analyze the motives of those who helped put him in power. If they labored for love of the new Prince, all well and good. If not, and they merely hated the deposed Prince, then the new one must take guard. Such men cannot be pleased, for malcontents rarely are. Rather, the Prince should seek support from those who previously backed his enemy. Such men will work hard for his love, and since they are of the habit of being content, will more easily support the new regime.

It has been customary for princes to construct fortresses in order to hold their states, and as a refuge in case of attack. Machiavelli approves of this, not because it is wise but rather because it is customary. He notes that Niccolò Vitelli destroyed two fortresses in Citta di Castello in order to retain that state, and the Duke of Urbino, after returning to his state from abroad, destroyed all the fortresses of his province. The Bentivogli, on returning to Bologna, took similar measures. So, the author concludes, fortresses may not be as useful as people think. They may aid one ruler and harm the other.

How may the Prince decide whether or not to have such fortresses? Machiavelli thinks that the Prince who fears his own people more than foreigners should construct fortresses, but the one who has greater fear of foreigners may do without them. The Sforza castle in Milan, he predicts, will cause that family trouble and disorder. The best fortress is the love of the people. Stone fortresses will not help the Prince if his subjects hate him. If the Prince is attacked, and he is loved, he will not need a stone fortress, for his people will rise in his defense. Machiavelli can think of only a few instances in which a fortress has aided the ruler of a state, and then it was used to protect the Prince against his own people.

Machiavelli concludes by praising those who built fortresses, and those who did not. He adds that the presence of such fortresses in the domain of the wise Prince indicates that he does not trust his people.

COMMENT: Machiavelli is convinced that the Prince, if he is wise, will rely more on the manipulation of men than on the construction of war machines. *The Prince*, though it deals with war, is more an essay on the nature of man. This is one of the lessons of Chapter XX: the Prince who deals wisely with men need not concern himself unduly with fortresses. The presence of such buildings in a state is a sign of some failure on the part of the Prince. Note that the first part of the chapter deals with the means by which the Prince may gain the support of territory newly captured. Should the Prince fail in Machiavelli's plan, then and only then would the author approve the construction of fortresses.

[handwritten margin notes:] dealings wisely w/ men

[handwritten bottom note:] fear + respect → NOT HATE

CHAPTER XXI

In this chapter, Machiavelli returns to the use of generalizations without relying strongly on examples and historical analysis. He is concerned with the reputation of the Prince. The reader will recall that in Chapter XVIII the author opened his discussion on the subject. Thus, this chapter may be viewed as an extension and elaboration of points made previously.

The Prince will gain great esteem if he engages successfully in important enterprises. As an example, Machiavelli offers the case of King Ferdinand of Aragon. He may be considered a new Prince, for he began his career as a weak ruler and soon transformed himself into the strongest king in Christendom. All of his actions were great and extraordinary. He was able to conquer Granada, while occupying the barons of Castile with other enterprises. He maintained his armies with Church money, a practice that Machiavelli strongly urged in a previous chapter.

His long and successful wars gave Ferdinand a brilliant reputation. Under the pretext of serving his religion, the King expelled the Moors from his domain and confiscated their holdings. Ferdinand also attacked Africa under the same pretext, and then invaded Italy and France. All of these spectacular accomplishments have astonished his people, who haven't had the time to organize against him.

> COMMENT: It is interesting to note that Machiavelli does not mention the voyages of Columbus at this point. These were financed by Ferdinand and Isabella, and were considered important at that time. Such non-European matters did not interest Machiavelli, whose sole ambition was the unification of Italy. Machiavelli was not a true example of the Renaissance man in this. He showed little interest in the arts or music, and concentrated all his interests on the one area of political action.

It is well for the Prince to have many impressive military victories, but he must also take care to demonstrate his greatness in internal affairs as well. Whenever one of his subjects does something extraordinary, either good or evil, he must be rewarded or punished. The other citizens will discuss the Prince's actions in such affairs, and will seek to imitate the good actions in order to gain rewards, and avoid the evil to prevent pain and punishment. "And above all, a Prince must endeavor in every action to obtain fame for being great and excellent."

A prince gains esteem when he is unreservedly in favor of someone or equally opposed to someone else. Such a policy is far better than remaining neutral. What if two neighboring states go to war against each other? After the war is over, the Prince will either have reason to fear the winner, or will not. In either case, it would be better for the Prince to declare himself openly and enter the war. If he remains neutral, he will fall prey to the victor, and this will please the defeated power. So, the Prince will be conquered by the one and will not receive aid from the other. The winner will not want friends whom he suspects, and neutrals are always suspected. The loser will not desire the Prince's friendship, for he was not given aid when it was most needed. *Do not stay Neutral*

Machiavelli offers an example of this. Antiochus was sent to Greece by the Aetolians to expel the Romans. He sent envoys to the Achaeian friends of Rome, who encouraged them to remain neutral in the coming struggle. At the same time, Roman envoys asked the Achaeians to join with them in the war. Both sides were present when the Achaeian council debated the matter. At this time, the Roman envoy said that if the Achaeians did not enter the war, they would become "without any favor or any reputation, the prize of the victor." Machiavelli indicates that he agrees with this analysis.

The Prince will always find that those who are not his friends will want him to remain neutral, while his friends will ask him to take arms. Irresolute princes, attempting to avoid dangers, will usually choose neutrality, and will be ruined by such a position. But the wise Prince will declare himself frankly for one side or the other. If the side to which the Prince joins himself wins, then it will be in his debt In a touch of rare idealism, Machiavelli states that "men are never so dishonest as to oppress you with such a patent ingratitude." More characteristically, he adds that the victor never emerges as strong as he expected from a battle, and he will need allies, and so keep the Prince's friendship. If the ally should lose, the Prince will still be assisted, for he will be needed in the future counterattack. In addition, such an ally is a good one to have. He needs the Prince more than the Prince needs him. He exists at the Prince's discretion, and cannot win without his aid.

Never ally yourself to one who is more powerful In this respect, the Prince should never ally himself with a ruler who is more powerful than himself. If he wins, the Prince will be in his power, and this must be avoided. The Venetians joined with France against the Duke of Milan, and this led to their ruin. When France defeated Milan, she gained control of Venice. Sometimes the Prince will not be able to avoid such a situation. This occurred when the Pope and the Spanish King attacked Lombardy. At that time, Florence was obliged to join the attackers. All policies are risky, says Machiavelli, and the Prince must choose the wisest. One never avoids one difficulty without running into another. The wise man understands the nature of the difficulties, and chooses the least harmful of them.

The Prince must also indicate his appreciation of merit, and reward excellence in all things. He must urge his people to follow their

callings in order to encourage respect for law. They should not
fear the loss of their goods through the instrumentality of the
Prince. Rather, those who better their state should receive recognition and rewards. The Prince should sponsor fairs and festivals,
at which he should appear and mingle with the people. This will
be a striking example of his generosity and humanity, which the
people will appreciate. He must be sure, however, that he does
nothing to detract from his majesty and dignity, and must never
fail in anything he does.

> **COMMENT:** Machiavelli makes two points in this chapter:
> the Prince must give the appearance of great strength, and
> he must never waver in choosing sides in a war. The Prince
> who shows weakness to his people will encourage them to
> conspire against him. The Prince who refuses to take sides in
> a war will suffer no matter which side wins. Although this
> chapter is essentially philosophical, it has a special meaning
> for Lorenzo, who remained neutral in several wars. Machia-
> velli wants this particular Prince to play a more aggressive role
> in Italian affairs than he has in the past. Only in this way
> can Italy be unified and the foreigners driven from the land.

CHAPTER XXII

In this chapter and the one that follows, Machiavelli attempts to
deal with what may appear to be minor problems which the Prince
must face. The major discussions on the problems facing princes
are to be found in Chapters XIX to XXI. In a sense, Chapters
XXII and XXIII tie up the loose ends regarding these questions.

The Prince's ministers vary as to quality. They are important not
only for the skills they may possess, but also because the impression of the Prince is based in large part on the reputation of his
ministers. When they are competent and faithful, the Prince is
thought of as being wise, since he has recognized their abilities,
and these men of quality are loyal to him. When they are neither
competent nor faithful, the Prince's reputation suffers.

Antonio da Venafro, the minister of Pandolfo Petrucci, the Prince
of Siena, was a wise and able man, and Pandolfo gained part of
his reputation for having employed such a minister. There are
three kinds of brains: one that understands things without assistance, one that understands things if they are pointed out by others,
and one that cannot understand matters even when they are
pointed out carefully. The first is best, the second is acceptable,
and the third is useless in ministers. It was evident that Pandolfo,
even if not of the first kind, was at least of the second. Even if the
Prince cannot originate brilliant thoughts and schemes, he should
have the ability to recognize them when presented by a first-rate
ministerial brain. In addition, if the Prince displays such judgment,
the wise minister will not attempt to deceive him.

There is a method by which the Prince may know his minister. If the minister has a greater impression of himself than of the Prince, and attempts to further his own ambitions against those of the Prince, then he will never become a good minister, and cannot be relied upon. The good minister must never think of his own welfare, but instead must concern himself solely with the well-being of the Prince. On the other hand, the wise Prince, to maintain the loyalty of a good minister, must reward him, do him kindnesses and grant him honors. Such treatment will contain his ambition, and make him fearful of losing what he has already gained. When the Prince and his minister have this relationship, there exists an atmosphere of mutual trust. Where this does not exist, both men suffer.

COMMENT: This short chapter seems rather pointless and obvious at first glance. But the reader must keep in mind the purpose of *The Prince*. Machiavelli hopes that Lorenzo will read it, and then call the author to Florence to become his chief minister. So, in this chapter, Machiavelli indicates what he expects his relationship with his future employer to be. He will serve the Prince well, and will expect to be rewarded for loyal and able service. On his part, he expects Lorenzo to be a wise Prince, and recognize the values of an able and loyal minister. There is still one more point to be noted. Lorenzo may fear his own judgment, and may not desire an ambitious man like Machiavelli in his court. These fears need not exist. The wise Prince need not have a first-rate brain. All he needs is the ability to recognize first-class brains in his ministers. Since the third alternative is the man with no brains at all, and since Lorenzo certainly does not fit into that category, the two men will be safe with each other, and both will prosper as a result of their collaboration.

CHAPTER XXIII

Before ending his discussion on the actions of the Prince, the author turns to a mistake the wise Prince must learn to avoid: he must not fall victim to flatterers. Courts are full of such men, and since all want to believe the best of themselves, flatterers are difficult to ignore. The only way the Prince may avoid this danger is to make it clear that he will not be offended if his followers speak the truth about him. On the other hand, if all feel they may tell the Prince the truth, they will lose their respect for him. A wise prince will take a course between these two extremes. He will choose for his ministers only wise men, and these will be given permission to speak the truth and avoid flattery. However, they will speak in that way only on subjects specified by the Prince. After hearing the councils of his ministers, the Prince should discuss and deliberate his problems with great care. The ministers will then note that the more openly they give their opinions, the more seriously they will be taken. As a result, they will be encouraged to speak their minds in the future. The Prince should listen to none other than these ministers, and be determined in his decisions. Whoever acts in another fashion either acts without care through flattery or else changes his mind too often, and if either of these two reasons is the cause of his actions, he will lose esteem.

Machiavelli then discusses the case of Pre' Luca, a follower of Maximilian, who said that the Emperor never consulted anyone, and yet never acted on his own instincts or decisions. The Emperor was a secretive man, and did not tell his plans to anyone or take anyone's advice. As soon as he put a plan into operation, it would be opposed by his followers, who then diverted the Emperor from the plan. Whatever Maximilian did one day he undid the next, and so lost his reputation.

A Prince should take counsel, but only when he desires it and not when others wish to volunteer advice. Indeed, he should go so far as to discourage his followers from giving him unrequested advice. But should he ask advice, he should ponder it carefully. If he finds that one of his ministers is not frank with him, the Prince should be angry. "It is an infallible rule that a prince who is not wise himself cannot be well advised, unless by chance he leaves himself entirely in the hands of one man who rules him in everything, and happens to be a prudent man." In such a case he may be well-governed, but in time the adviser will take control of his state. Should the Prince ask the opinion of many, and they are not frank, he will not receive the same advice. Each counselor will offer a different opinion, and each will think of his own interests. Men will always be false unless they are compelled to be true. So it is that wise counsels, if and when they are granted, are granted only to a wise Prince.

> **COMMENT:** This concludes Machiavelli's advice to Princes as to their actions. Once again, he is addressing Lorenzo. He says that he does not want sole power; indeed, he warns against advisers who are in such a position. Instead, he promises that he will not hide the truth from the Prince. What that truth is, Machiavelli discusses in the remaining chapters of the book.

CHAPTER XXIV

Up to this point, Machiavelli has discussed the various types of princes and how they may overcome obstacles and take advantage of opportunities. If one may view *The Prince* as both a book of political philosophy and a guide for Lorenzo, it can be deduced that Machiavelli discusses the first aspect while only alluding to the second. He hopes that Lorenzo will profit from his maxims, but he does not spell out the ways by which this may be done. In this chapter, and for the rest of the book, Machiavelli gets down to brass tacks. Although still discussing ancient and modern examples, and putting forth maxims, he openly calls upon his Prince to lead a movement for the unification of Italy. As a result, Machiavelli concentrates on the problems of new princes, for the future ruler of Italy will face more of these problems than any other.

Machiavelli begins by observing that if the new Prince follows his suggestions, he will have even more power than an old, established ruler. This is so because a new Prince is watched more carefully than an old one. If his actions are good, they are quickly noted and greatly appreciated. "For men are much more taken by present than by past things, and when they find themselves well off in the present, they enjoy it and seek nothing more." So it is that the new Prince who succeeds has the double glory of founding a state and then ruling it well. Similarly, the new Prince who fails suffers a double shame.

If one studies those princes who have lost their power in recent years, one notes immediately that they all suffered through a lack of arms. Some had to face hostile populations. Others, who had friendly populations, lacked the trust and support of the nobles. Without these defects, these rulers would surely have survived. Machiavelli notes that Philip of Macedon (he is not referring here to the father of Alexander the Great, but another ruler with the same name) did not possess a great state, but was able to earn the support of the people and the nobles. In addition, he was a military man. Although Philip did lose some cities to his enemies, his kingdom remained intact.

Because of this, princes who have lost their kingdoms after having controlled them for a number of years cannot blame bad luck for their losses. Instead, it was probably their own fault. They should have realized in good times that bad times can come. When troubles arose, they thought of fleeing instead of standing and defending their domains. They then hoped that the people, angered by foreign attacks, would support them. This may be true, but it will not be enough if the Prince has ignored the other factors. The Prince should not rely on others to pick him up once he falls. This may happen, but it is hardly to be depended upon. "Only those defences are good, certain, and durable, which depend on yourself alone and your own ability."

COMMENT: There is nothing new in this chapter, which may be viewed as a transition from Machiavelli's discussion of the qualities of princes to his call to arms. It should be noted that this last section of the book begins quietly. In succeeding chapters, Machiavelli will combine political and philosophical analysis with a semi-religious call to arms. Thus, this opening chapter may be viewed as a prelude.

CHAPTER XXV

Machiavelli opens this chapter by saying, "It is not unknown to me how many have been and are of the opinion that worldly events are so governed by fortune and by God, that men cannot by their prudence change them." These people leave all to chance, feeling that they lack the power to change events preordained by the deities. Machiavelli will return to this point, which he does not accept entirely, to demonstrate that God offers man several alternatives and leaves it to him to choose the wise one. In this respect, the Prince may combine a semi-religious calling with the strength and shrewdness of the lion and the fox.

Machiavelli goes on to say that the belief in the inability of man to alter God's plan is held by many men in his own time. In thinking about the problem, he is inclined to accept some of their arguments. Nevertheless, free will must also be taken into account. "I think it may be that fortune is the ruler of half our actions, but that she allows the other half or thereabouts to be governed by us." The author compares fortune to a wild river that may destroy all in its path. Yet, when it is quiet, wise men can erect dikes and banks, so that when it rises again it will not destroy the countryside. In this way, man may control the forces of nature and, the author suggests, may direct God's will. To be sure that the Prince recognizes what he is saying, Machiavelli adds that Italy has been a country without dikes or banks. If she had been as well-protected as Germany, France and Spain, she would not have suffered as much.

Some princes seem fortunate today, but are ruined tomorrow. The princes have not changed, but their conditions have been altered drastically. Machiavelli believes this is caused by the problems discussed previously. The Prince who bases his power solely on fortune is ruined once his fortune has changed. Machiavelli also believes that the happy Prince is one whose actions follow the needs of the times, and unhappy princes go against the needs of the times. Men who seek glory and riches may take different paths to reach their goals. One may proceed with caution, another with rashness. Some use violence while others rely on cunning. One man may be patient, while another may be impatient. One cautious man may succeed, while another with the same quality may fail. Two men who are completely opposed as to methods may both have success.

Machiavelli concludes that each man must act in such a way as to be in harmony with the needs of the problem. Some conditions may call for one method of approach while others call for the opposite. Thus, the wise Prince must be adaptable and sense the temper of the times. This is difficult to carry out, for the Prince who has been successful by being cautious will not easily be persuaded to be rash once conditions have been changed. Further, cautious men often find it impossible to act rashly, and vice versa. Such rigid princes will have difficulty maintaining their power. If the Prince could learn to change when conditions change, his fortune would remain constant. Thus, one's fortune never changes, but rather one's context develops. If the Prince does not also develop within the context, he is doomed.

Pope Julius II was a most impetuous man, and because the times called for such a quality he prospered. This could be seen in his first war against Bologna. Venice and Spain did not support him in this conflict, and France also indicated a reluctance to accept the Papal position. In spite of this, Julius went ahead and fought Bologna on his own. His rashness caused Venice to hesitate because of fear and Spain to refrain from acting in the hope of recovering Naples after the war. France was obliged to support Julius, for the King of France wanted Papal support in his struggle with Venice. So, Julius achieved what no other Pope in history had achieved because he was bold. If he had waited to organize an alliance, he never would have succeeded. The French King would have found thousands of excuses not to join in the war, while the others would have inspired him with a thousand fears. All of the Pope's actions showed his impetuous nature, and he succeeded in all he did because the times called for such a man. On the other hand, had Julius lived a little longer and attempted his conquests when the times called for caution, he surely would have failed.

Machiavelli concludes that man and fortune are both variables. Success is achieved when they are in harmony; when they are not, failure is certain. Nonetheless, Machiavelli believes that it is better to be bold than it is to be cautious. Fortune is a woman, and if the Prince would master her, he must be prepared to conquer her by force if necessary. Fortune prefers to be taken by forceful men, and looks upon the cautious with disdain. "And therefore, like a woman, she is always a friend to the young, because they are less cautious, fiercer, and master her with greater audacity."

COMMENT: At the beginning of the chapter, Machiavelli indicates that what other men call God, he calls fortune, chance, or even luck. Machiavelli refers to this quality as virtú. To Machiavelli, virtú consists of harmony with natural law. To say that the gods enable one man to succeed and the other to fail is senseless in his view of things. The Prince—meaning Lorenzo—must not be deluded by such nonsense, which will only lead to his destruction. Instead, he must make use of the opportunities presented to him along the way to his unification of Italy. There were several major powers in Italy at the time, and Florence was by no means a first-class military state. Thus, Machiavelli urges Lorenzo to be bold, for if he is, he can win without a great massing of strength. This is why he introduces the case of Pope Julius. When in doubt, act boldly, is his advice. On the other hand, the Prince must be prepared to shift tactics at a moment's notice.

CHAPTER XXVI

This chapter is entitled: "Exhortation to Liberate Italy from the Barbarians." In it, Machiavelli sums up *The Prince*, both as a study of politics and as a call to arms. In this respect, the final chapter is both a conclusion and a rallying cry.

Machiavelli believes that the time is ripe for a new Prince to conquer and unify Italy. In a series of examples, he indicates that Lorenzo may follow the great men of history in this task. Moses could not show his talents until the people of Israel were reduced by the Egyptians. A Cyrus could arise only after the Persians were enslaved by the Medes. Similarly, until the Athenians were conquered, Theseus could not set them free. So it is that the true glory of the Italian liberator cannot be recognized until Italy is hopelessly destroyed. This, says the author, is the situation at present. Italy is more enslaved than the Hebrews, more oppressed than the Persians, and more scattered than the Athenians. The nation is without a head, "without order, beaten, despoiled, lacerated, and overrun," and has suffered ruins of every kind. In this way, Machiavelli all but says outright that Lorenzo may have the fortune and opportunity of a Moses; like the Hebrew leader, he may become the instrument of God.

Once before, it appeared as though God had selected a Prince as his instrument in the unification of Italy (Machiavelli is referring to Cesare Borgia). Yet this individual, after having reached the summit of his career, was thrown aside by fortune. The author implies that Cesare did not follow the advice he would give to Lorenzo. Italy now awaits a savior, who will put a stop to the destruction of Lombardy, to the mismanagement in Naples and Tuscany, and cure the nation of its other ills. The nation prays to God for a deliverer. She is ready to follow any standard that may be raised. The one best hope of Italy is Lorenzo, and Machiavelli implores this Prince to heed the call. The Medicis are favored by God and the Church; they must not ignore the call. And it will not be difficult to win the objectives, if Lorenzo follows the guidelines set down in this book, and follows the actions and lives of the men mentioned in its pages.

These men were truly great, but they were, after all, only men. Each had less opportunity for greatness than has Lorenzo. Their enterprises were not juster or easier than his, and God was no more on their side than He is on that of Lorenzo. If Lorenzo is willing to undertake the task, he can accomplish it. In addition, if God is on his side, there may be miracles as well; "the sea has been opened, a cloud has shown you the road, the rock has given forth water, manna has rained, and everything has contributed to your greatness." The rest is left to Lorenzo. God will not do everything, but his assistance may be counted on.

Lorenzo should not wonder that none of his predecessors has been able to unify Italy. Their methods have been at fault, and not their will and bravery. They lacked the opportunity to learn new methods. Machiavelli implies that they lacked him as an adviser. A new Prince gains more honors from his new laws and measures than from anything else he may do. Italy offers a wide scope for new ideas. This lack of ideas has been the major problem of Lorenzo's predecessors. Italians are stronger than all others in individual duels; they do not lack dexterity, strength, and intelligence. But when fighting in armies, they made poor showings. This is because their leaders have been weak, and those who have intelligence have not been able to win the support of the people. So it has been that every time an Italian army fights without allies, it loses.

If Lorenzo would unify Italy, he must make certain his armies are strong and loyal. If such armies are led by a strong and beloved leader, their strength will be greatly increased. The Swiss and Spanish infantries are considered unbeatable, but they have their defects, which can be exploited. The Spaniards cannot meet a cavalry charge, and the Swiss fear combat with determined men. Machiavelli then offers examples of how and when these great forces were overcome. If the Prince knows their defects, he can form a force that can resist cavalry and need not fear infantry. He will have to choose his arms with care, and organize well. If these measures are taken, they will give reputation and grandeur to the Prince.

The opportunity must not be allowed to pass. Machiavelli cannot find words to express the love such a liberator would receive from his countrymen. "What doors would be closed to him? What people would refuse him obedience? What envy could oppose him? What Italian would withhold allegiance?" The domination by foreigners (Machiavelli calls them barbarians) "stinks in the nostrils of all." The author hopes the Medicis will heed this call and take this opportunity. He closes by quoting Petrarch:

> Valor against fell wrath
> Will take up arms; and be the combat quickly sped!
> For sure, the ancient worth,
> That in Italians stirs the heart, is not yet dead.

COMMENT: There is a great deal of contention among scholars regarding this final chapter in *The Prince*. Machiavelli, who shows little emotion in other parts of the book, concludes with a final burst of patriotic bombast. There are several possible explanations for this apparent switch in style: (1) Machiavelli tries to indicate that he recognizes the immorality of many of his suggestions and hopes to show that the end is so noble and important that any means to attain it will be purified; (2) it was added in the style of other similar exhortations of the period that were addressed to princes of the Italian Renaissance; (3) it was added later, as an afterthought; (4) Machiavelli feared that Lorenzo would not be able to see through the masked suggestions offered elsewhere in the work, so he spelled out his proposal in detail; (5) Machiavelli hoped that, should Lorenzo not accept his offer of assistance, the book would be read by another Prince, who might.

DISCOURSES ON THE
FIRST TEN BOOKS OF TITUS LIVIUS

Most scholars believe that Machiavelli wrote *The Prince* as an interruption to his larger work, *The Discourses*. According to this interpretation, Machiavelli intended *The Discourses* as his great statement of belief, while *The Prince* was written as his bid for a position in Lorenzo's court. While this view has much merit, it should be noted that there are many points of similarity between the two works. Both reflect Machiavelli's essential philosophy of life and history. Both tend to ignore the non-political side of life, and the author's conviction that man acts through self-interest can be found in each of the works. In other words, the two books show Machiavelli's stamp clearly; the morality of *The Discourses* is the same as that of *The Prince*.

On the other hand, there are several differences to be noted. There is a greater stress on philosophy in *The Prince*, and more of an attempt to write conventional history in *The Discourses*. The former work presents maxims, which are then supported by a few historical examples. In the latter, Machiavelli wrote a history of the Roman Republic from its origins to the middle of the third century, and from this body of happenings, drew several conclusions. It may be said, then, that *The Prince* was written by the political philosopher and *The Discourses* by the historian. Further, in *The Prince*, Machiavelli has written a guide to actions in the present, and often disregards the historical record or manipulates it. *The Discourses* was written with no such intent and therefore can be free of the author's own version of "Machiavellian tactics." This is not to say that Machiavelli does not believe the present generation cannot learn from the past, or apply its lessons in the present. Rather, these points must be drawn from between the lines in *The Discourses*; they are not spelled out in the fashion of *The Prince*.

Machiavelli bases his work on the first ten books of Titus Livius (Livy), the great historian of Rome's period of glory. On the other hand, he does not follow the Roman exactly. For example, Livy's books on the second century have been lost, and Machiavelli was obliged to imagine the Roman's view toward this period. In addition, there is little mention of Livy in *The Discourses*, which leads the reader to assume that his books were picked as a starting point and reference, and for no other reason. Why, then, did Machiavelli choose this period to write about? There are several possible answers to this question, and the answer can probably be found in most of them. In the first place, during the Renaissance it was common to look to the ancients for advice and example; by writing of Rome, Machiavelli was only following the accepted customs of his day. Secondly, the history of Rome is one of the rise of a small city-state into the position of ruler of the world.

It is the author's hope that the reader will note that an Italian city-state, such as Florence, may imitate Rome in this accomplishment. On the other hand, Machiavelli does not suppose that the ancients were superior to the moderns. They made mistakes, had less knowledge than the Renaissance men, and therefore must not be looked upon as the ultimate guides. Indeed, early in the work, Machiavelli indicates his belief that the rulers of Egypt and other pre-Hellenic civilizations are much more to be admired than the Romans. Thirdly, the history of Rome offers many examples whereby strong rulers using powerful armies were able to take control of large amounts of territory. In addition, the Roman genius for administration, present during the Republic as well as the Empire that followed, offers many areas of commentary for the author. In this respect, *The Discourses* offers as many opportunities for discussions of the arts of leadership as *The Prince*. In Chapter IV, for example, we read a sentence such as this one: "It cannot be denied that the Roman Empire was the result of good fortune and military discipline; but it seems to me that it ought to be perceived that where good discipline prevails there also will good order prevail, and good fortune rarely fails to follow in their tracks." Thus, in this work as in *The Prince*, Machiavelli stresses the necessity for the ruler to have good fortune and at the same time exploit his opportunities for power.

A fourth and final reason for the use of Roman history to present the author's ideas is the role of the Church in Roman history. Like many figures of the Renaissance, Machiavelli thought the Empire was undermined by the Church. This is a major reason for his continuing *The Discourses* beyond the limits of Livy's known works. Machiavelli seems to be saying that just as the Church destroyed the Republic, so it is standing in the way of modern Italian greatness by blocking the unification of Italy.

The Discourses is not as meaty as *The Prince*; there are stretches in the book where the author seems to be rambling, and these could easily be cut and ignored. It should be remembered that *The Discourses* is five times as long as *The Prince*. One cannot expect a work of this length to burn fiercely with ideas on every page, as *The Prince* does. In addition, as has been noted, there are no truly important ideas discussed in *The Discourses* that are not to be found in one form or another in the shorter work.

What are the ideas to be found in *The Discourses?* And what lessons are to be learned from the experience of the Roman Republic? In the first place, Machiavelli makes it quite clear that the most effective governments rest on firm popular support. He admires the Roman Republic for developing the types of institutions whereby the people's will and desires can be expressed. These factors are also discussed in *The Prince*, again showing the similarity in viewpoints between the two works. It is for this reason that Machiavelli considers the democratic republic to be the best

form of government yet devised. Under other forms, the Prince
may never be sure of mass support. Thus, even a despot must
attempt to win the approval of the multitudes. This sentiment
can also be found in Machiavelli's stress on stability and harmony
in *The Prince*. If the state is in turmoil, the ruler can scarcely be
expected to engage in foreign adventures. This stability may be
achieved in many ways, and one of the most important of these is
the establishment of a national religion, which will clearly be
subservient to the state and obey the Prince in all he desires.

A second lesson to be learned from Rome concerns the role of the
ruling class in the Republic. Machiavelli believes that Rome could
never have achieved its greatness if it were not for the quality
and quantity of extraordinary men in its population. In this respect, it is well to note that the great Romans mentioned in *The
Discourses* all show the same qualities as those described in *The
Prince*. The Prince must be adept at war; were it not for the
warlike proclivities of the Romans, says the author, the Republic
might have gone down the drain as many other small states of the
period did. In this regard, it was well that Roman religion during
the Republic did not stress pacifist values. Instead, the pagan
religions of the Republic were all geared to what would today
be called brutal values. This may be considered a key point that
The Discourses and *The Prince* share; both offer strong indictments
of Christianity in one aspect or another. In *The Prince*, Machiavelli argues that the Church is responsible in large part for the
sorry state of Italian politics, for having refused to unite Italy
when it had the power. In *The Discourses*, the author condemns
Christianity for sapping the strength of the Republic by preaching
pacifism, the value of charity, and the obligation of the strong to
aid the weak. When soldiers become true Christians, they cease
to be soldiers. Further, the new Church, unlike the pagan religions, did not support the policies of the Republic. Thus, the
Catholic Church in embryo destroyed the Republic, and in ma-
turity blocked the unification of Italy.

A third lesson derived from *The Discourses* is both implicit and
explicit in the work; Machiavelli the historian believes that history
moves in cycles. Civilizations rise when they find their proper
spirit, achieve unity, and propel proper leaders to the fore. Then,
in success, they become decadent, and those qualities that made
for greatness at an earlier time are forgotten and discarded. It is
this corruption of Roman civilization, both by its success and the
effects of Christianity, that led to the downfall of the Republic
and the rise of the Empire.

Similarly, Machiavelli feels that the Empire followed this pattern,
and he implies that modern Italy may suffer the same fate. This
is not to say that the Church is condemned in *The Discourses;* on
the contrary, he expresses great admiration for Church leaders
who, after all, resembled his model Prince in many respects. If

Christianity could conquer the great Roman Empire without an army, it certainly cannot be dismissed lightly. Machiavelli hopes that the reader may derive important examples from the history of the early Church. In a way, he is imitating the early Christian leaders. If they could bring about the downfall of Rome with words, perhaps he can unify Italy with the same weapon. In *The Discourses*, Machiavelli professes admiration for Fabius, the general who used delaying tactics and slow maneuvering in the second Punic War and triumphed over Hannibal. He observes that Fabius was much wiser than the brash general Decius. Both men won triumphs, but Fabius survived while Decius died. Thus, he implies that the failure of the Church lay not in its methods and tactics, but in its goals.

Finally, it must be noted that both works exhibit a strong support of republics for their own sake as well as a means to the end of conquest and power. This is to say that republics, as opposed to tyrannies and despotisms, are ends as well as means. Machiavelli has the reputation of despising people, believing little but ill of mankind, and of thinking that the masses deserve the ill fortune they have fallen to in Italy. Nothing could be further from the truth. If Machiavelli truly believed these things, why would he spend his time writing works aimed at the unification of his country by a popular leader? If personal ambition were his only drive, he could have achieved positions in other courts instead of wasting his time in an agonizing exile. The reader must always keep in mind the fact that the desired end for Machiavelli was always a strong, unified Italy, and not power for its own sake. This overriding fact is often forgotten, especially by those who read of "Machiavellism," and ignore the man and his writings. Perhaps this is because Machiavelli wrote of the situation as it was, and not as it should be. Machiavelli loved Italy in spite of and often because of its problems, and not for some romantic vision that had little chance of being attained.

MACHIAVELLI'S OTHER WORKS
AND HIS LATER LIFE

Although Machiavelli is best known for *The Prince,* and to a lesser extent *The Discourses,* these are by no means his only important literary works. Many of his letters survive. Some tell of his plans, others are requests for positions or advice to rulers, and several tell of his boredom in exile. The latter, while they tell little of Machiavelli the political philosopher, demonstrate another side of Machiavelli the man, who was a sensualist in an age of sensualism. Some of these letters, which deal with Machiavelli's sexual activities, border on the pornographic and show a man bedeviled by problems of the flesh, as the political works show a man concerned with those of the mind.

This side of Machiavelli is also seen in *Mandragola,* which was considered an outstanding comedy of the Renaissance stage, and was written around 1518. The play deals with a Florentine named Callimaco, who, on hearing of the beauty of Lucrezia, the wife of Nicias, decides he must seduce her. After surveying the situation, Callimaco decides on his course of action. The married couple would like very much to have children, but Lucrezia has failed to conceive. Although by nature a modest woman, Lucrezia makes it clear that she will undergo any pain in order to have children. Callimaco arranges to be introduced to her as a physician who has drugs that will make any woman fertile. However, the first man who sleeps with a woman who has taken the drugs will die. Callimaco bravely offers to give the drugs to Lucrezia and then sacrifice himself by sleeping with her. Nicias is agreeable to this sacrifice, but Lucrezia says she does not want to commit adultery and murder with the same act. But her mother is all for the plan, and she bribes Lucrezia's confessor to support it as well. Lucrezia finally agrees to go through with it, takes the drug, and sleeps with Callimaco. As a result, she becomes pregnant. The play ends with everyone in a state of bliss. Nicias and Lucrezia look forward to the birth of their child, the priest forgives Lucrezia her transgressions, and Callimaco announces that now he will be able to sleep nights again.

Mandragola was an instant hit, and Pope Leo X in particular enjoyed it. He suggested that Machiavelli might be employed to write a history of Florence, and soon after the author was given the commission.

The History of Florence was begun in 1520 and completed in 1525. Despite its many defects, it remains an important work both in understanding Machiavelli and in the history of historical writing. The author ignores the myths that were so often found in earlier works. He is interested in telling the true history of the state and not in putting out a piece of propaganda. In its pages we find the same philosophy that had previously been stated in *The Prince* and

The Discourses. Machiavelli repeats his belief that the Church bears the major share of guilt in Italy's sad situation. In order to preserve its small empire in central Italy, the Papacy has conspired to prevent the unification of the entire peninsula into a single powerful state that would have been dominated by others. The heroes of the book—Theodoric, Cosimo de Medici, and Lorenzo de Medici—all follow the pattern of the successful leader as set forth in *The Prince*. *The History of Florence* contains selections in which Machiavelli's heroes are shown to gain the trust of the population, choose their advisers with care, and learn the arts of war thoroughly. The author remarks on the fickleness of the masses and suggests how they may be controlled. Toward the end of the work we find a passionate call for national unity reminiscent of the closing chapter of *The Prince*.

Similarly, Machiavelli's other important work, *The Art of War*, may be viewed as a commentary on *The Prince*. In each of the seven books of this work, the author echoes the military advice given in earlier volumes. If the reader has carefully gone over chapters XII and XIII of *The Prince*, he will find little new in *The Art of War*. There is, however, one interesting flash of Machiavelli's genius to be found in its pages. Machiavelli probably never witnessed a battle in which firearms played a decisive role. They were used effectively in the battle of Marignano, but Machiavelli could not have known much of this encounter. Nonetheless, he predicts that firearms will have a decisive effect on future wars and encourages the wise military leader to learn of their uses and arm himself with the latest equipment. Some scholars go so far as to say that Machiavelli, in addition to being one of the founders of modern political science, also was among the first to lay the foundations for modern military science.

In 1525, while completing his work on *The History of Florence*, Machiavelli found time to send letters of advice to Pope Clement VII, who was besieged by Emperor Charles V, whose Spanish and German armies were in the process of conquering Italy. As the Emperor's armies appeared before Florence, Machiavelli was recalled to the city and, at the Pope's request, drew up a plan of defense that reflected ideas to be found in *The Art of War*. He was soon chosen to head a group known as "The Curators of the Walls," whose task it was to assure proper upkeep and defense of the walls around Florence. The German and Spanish armies did not attack Florence, but turned instead on Rome. The Pope was taken into custody, an act that inspired republican forces in Florence to revolt against the Medicis and restore the ancient republic. Hoping that his past services would be remembered, Machiavelli applied for his old position as secretary. His application was rejected; the Medicis had not trusted him for his republican background, and now the republicans denied him a post for his aid to the Medicis.

With this, Machiavelli returned to exile. He had lost his zest for
living after realizing that there was no hope of political posts in
Florence. His letters of this last exile reveal a man who lacked
almost all interest in public affairs. Machiavelli soon fell ill to
stomach disorders. He was 58 years old in 1527, an old man for
the times. Machiavelli died on June 22. In a letter to his brother,
his son Piero indicates that he may have repented in his last hours,
but most scholars, perhaps taking the true measure of the man,
doubt this.

> Pisa, June 22, 1527
>
> My dearest Francesco:
>
> I can only weep as I have to tell you that Niccolò, our
> father, died here on this 22nd of stomach pains caused by
> a medicine he took on the 20th. He allowed Brother
> Matteo, who was with him to the last, to hear his con-
> fession. Our father, as you know, left us in direst poverty.
> When you return this way, I shall have a great deal to
> tell you. Just now, I am in a hurry and will say no more.
> My best compliments.
>
> **Your Relative Piero Machiavelli**

CONTRASTING VIEWS ON
MACHIAVELLI

Machiavelli has been one of the most controversial figures in the history of political thought, and *The Prince* one of its most discussed works. The debate began during the author's life and continues to this day.

One of Machiavelli's closest friends, and the contemporary whose mind was perhaps most similar to his in operation, was Francesco Guicciardini, the author of a history of Florence that preceded and in some ways anticipated that of Machiavelli. Guicciardini accepted Machiavelli's views on human nature, the art of war, and the role of the Prince. He disagreed, however, on the role of the Church in Italian politics. It is true, he wrote, that the Church had prevented the unification of Italy. Further, domination of Italy by a single power would have brought glory to all Italians. On the other hand, such domination would also have destroyed all vestiges of liberty on the peninsula. "And divided Italy has succeeded in having so many free cities that I believe a single republic would have caused her more misery than happiness." According to Guicciardini, it is the Italian love of liberty, and not political problems, that prevent unification. "This land has always desired liberty, and therefore has never been able to unite under one rule."

Guicciardini's criticisms were mild compared with those that came after Machiavelli's death. As might have been expected, the Church placed Machiavelli's works on the Index, and Catholic writers, both before, during, and after the Reformation, attacked him for being amoral, immoral, and anti-Catholic. Cardinal Reginald Pole, writing in the *Apologia ad Carolum V. Caesarem*, contended that Machiavelli was an agent of the devil and *The Prince* proceeded from a hellish mind. Like other Church leaders, he charged that Protestant rulers, such as Henry VIII of Britain, were inspired by this anti-Catholic work.

The religious wars of the sixteenth century heightened interest in and hatred of Machiavelli. The French writer Innocent Gentillet wrote his famous *Contre-Machiavel* in 1571, as a bitter attack on every aspect of Machiavelli's works. All evil can be traced to *The Prince*, he claimed. Gentillet, a Huguenot, blamed the St. Bartholomew Day's Massacre on *The Prince*, and claimed that French foreign and domestic policy could be traced to its pages. For Gentillet, Machiavelli was guilty of "contempt of God, perfidy, sodomy, tyranny, cruelty, pillage, foreign usury, and other detestable vices." On the other hand, it should be noted that in some ways, Gentillet himself was a true Machiavellian; his book was dedicated to the Duke of Alençon, a friend of the Huguenots.

This picture of Machiavelli went swiftly from France to Britain. We find that Elizabethan drama was saturated with references to

Machiavelli. One scholar has discovered almost four hundred individual references to Machiavelli in the plays of this period. Shakespeare's Iago, in *Othello*, is usually considered that author's vision of the perfect Machiavellian. In the play, Iago says:

> For when my outward action doth demonstrate
> The native act and figure of my heart
> In compliment extern, 'tis not long after
> But I will wear my heart upon my sleeve
> For daws to peck at; I am not what I am.

Perhaps no ruler of the eighteenth century was more a Machiavellian than Frederick the Great of Prussia. Nonetheless, this King was the author of *Refutation of the Prince of Machiavelli*. As Voltaire later wrote: "The King of Prussia, some time before the death of his father, took it into his head to write a book against the principles of Machiavelli. If Machiavelli had had a prince for disciple, the first thing he would have recommended him to do would have been to write a book against Machiavellism." Frederick calls Machiavelli to task for praising evil men, misjudging the intelligence of people, and calling upon princes to be dishonest, amoral, and hypocritical. In a letter to Voltaire, he says that a writer who encourages men "to break their word, to oppress, to be unjust, even if he were a man remarkable for his intellectual attainments, should never be allowed to occupy the place reserved for those of praiseworthy and virtuous achievements." On the other hand, in a different letter, he asserts his belief that Voltaire did not admire Machiavelli's teachings, but accepted the Italian writer "only as a man of genius." Frederick carefully followed Machiavelli's teachings in his own life; Wyndham Lewis calls him "the last Machiavel in history no doubt that will ever be seen, or at least of which history will be allowed to preserve a true portrait."

Criticism of Machiavelli continued throughout the Enlightenment and the nineteenth century. To the man of the Enlightenment, Machiavelli's disregard of natural laws seemed unpardonable. To the French revolutionary, his concern for princes and apparent contempt for the masses could not be accepted. Napoleon privately praised *The Prince* and publicly condemned it. The mechanistic, deterministic nineteenth-century intellectual found little in the works of Machiavelli to praise, with the exception of nationalists, who found inspiration in his call for Italian unification. Among some Italians, he was considered the precursor of Cavour and Garibaldi.

Social Darwinists tended to ignore Machiavelli, but their rationales often sounded similar to those of the Italian writer. Some authors find echoes of Machiavelli in Georges Sorel and Friedrich Nietzsche. *The Prince*, like Nietzsche's superman, is thought to be beyond good and evil. This comparison is unfair to both men. Machiavelli considered the Prince to be bounded by rules; *The Prince* is nothing if not a book of rules. On the other hand, Nietzsche would have little but contempt for a writer who fawned, curried favor, and in other ways degraded himself. Nietzsche's Prince, if he had one, would have been direct and brutal, whereas Machiavelli's was devious and indirect, and used a rapier instead of a club on most occasions.

Machiavelli's reputation has undergone many revisions in the twentieth century. In many ways, he speaks to the present with a clearer and more familiar voice than any other Renaissance figure with the possible exception of Leonardo da Vinci. Machiavelli's overriding interest in nationalism appeals to an age in which nationalism has become the prime loyalty of most of the people of the world. His pragmatism has appeal to followers of that philosophy; some critics find in *The Prince* elements of existentialism as well. Machiavelli's political works, free from myth, have earned him the title of "father of political science" among some social scientists. The author's willingness to use almost any means to achieve his ends has direct appeal to many amoral leaders of today. Some psychologists find in his works deep insights as to the nature of man, and a recognition of unconscious drives. On the other hand, there are still those who find in *The Prince* a work of evil, a destructive philosophy, and maxims that, if applied, could lead to the destruction of the world. Finally, one critic believes Machiavelli was a great satirist, and *The Prince* a great joke the author was playing on his readers.

Machiavelli the nationalist is discussed by Pasquale Villari in his *The Life and Times of Machiavelli*. This work, which is one of the few good biographies of Machiavelli, concentrates on his work for Italian unification. Villari compares Machiavelli with Savonarola. The latter's ideas of a religious regeneration that could lead to a unified Italy were doomed to failure by the inactivity and disinterestedness of the Papacy. Thus, the example of German nationalism, led by Luther and his followers, could not work. Instead, the vision of Machiavelli—of an Italy united against the Church rather than by it—had to be used. Villari, writing in 1929, at a time when Mussolini's government had appeared to give Italy new vigor, stated: "At the present day, when Italy's political redemption has begun, and the nation is constituted according to the prophecies of Machiavelli, the moment has at last come for justice to be done to him."

Mussolini did not enshrine Machiavelli among the Italian patriots, however, for his government was strongly supported by the Church. Instead, Italian democratic nationalists, ignoring Machiavelli's apparent contempt for the masses, looked upon him as a precursor of Garibaldi. Writing in 1870, as "the bells are ringing throughout the land announcing the entry of Italians into Rome," Francesco de Sanctis echoed the shout, "Long live Italian unity! Glory to Machiavelli!" In 1930, Sir Richard Lodge wrote:

Although Machiavelli's dream was not realised, though no Medici aspired to play the role of Victor Emmanuel . . . his whole-hearted advocacy of his country's cause has never been forgotten, and ever since the middle of the last century he has stood higher in the estimation of his fellow-countrymen than at any other time since his death.

In a short work entitled *Machiavelli the Scientist,* by Leona Olschki, we read the assertion that "Machiavelli was the first theorist of statecraft who wrote about that subject from firsthand experience, both as a politician and as an historian." Further on, Olschki states that "by asking how principalities are won, how they are held or lost, Machiavelli transformed history into an empirical science and made of politics a system of universal rules." To Olschki, Machiavelli was the Galileo of the social sciences, whose axioms are still accepted. This view is supported by Ernst Cassirer, in *The Myth of the State.* Cassirer believes *The Prince* was basically a technical work, and that its author had "the coolness and indifference of a scientist." On the other hand, Joseph Kraft believes that "Machiavelli did not observe the facts closely. His deductions were, in many cases, illogical. He utterly misread the general military picture of the day." To Kraft, Machiavelli is more an artist than a scientist, more an ardent nationalist than a disinterested observer. In this regard, it should be noted that Cassirer calls Machiavelli a political artist rather than a political scientist. This is meant as a compliment, however.

Garrett Mattingly, the Renaissance scholar, wrote the most intriguing and radical interpretation of *The Prince* to appear in recent years. According to Mattingly, *The Prince* "contradicts everything else Machiavelli ever wrote and everything we know about his life." Machiavelli certainly realized that it would become a well-known work, and that it would be read by many besides Lorenzo. Considering the climate of the times, it could scarcely make the author many friends, and might lead to his demise. Such a development would be most un-Machiavellian of Machiavelli. Further, Machiavelli's family had a long history of opposition to the Medici, and Mattingly doubts the seriousness of the dedication. "I suppose it is possible to imagine that a man who has seen his country enslaved, his life's work wrecked and his own career with it, and has, for good measure, been tortured within an inch of his life should thereupon go home and write a book intended to teach his enemies the proper way to maintain themselves, writing all the time, remember, with the passionless objectivity of a scientist in a laboratory." Mattingly, however, cannot believe this. Instead, he holds that *The Prince* was a parody of many of the "mirrors for princes" published during his lifetime. These small works, designed to curry favor with rulers, were generally full of flattery and useless advice.

The intent of *The Prince* was to shock and not to instruct, Mattingly says. This should be evident to any student of the Renaissance. For example, contemporaries of Machiavelli would have realized that Cesare Borgia's life was full of mistakes and outright blunders, and would have known that Machiavelli would not choose him, of all people, as his model if the book were serious. Finally, Mattingly notes that Machiavelli's republican friends were not enraged by *The Prince*, and the author's letters to them continued as before. It should be noted that Mattingly's works on Machiavelli have been read with interest, but few scholars accept his theories. On the other hand, none have written criticisms of the Mattingly view. If it is correct, then all of the previous criticisms and analyses of *The Prince* will have to be re-written at best or discarded completely.

SAMPLE ESSAY QUESTIONS

1. In what respects was Machiavelli a "Renaissance man," and in what respects did he transcend his time and place?

There are two methods of judging a work of art, a book of history, or any other object from the past. The student can view it as a product of a particular mind that existed in a particular period, or he can try to appreciate it without regard to its period. For example, the viewer may gain great pleasure by reading a play by Shakespeare without knowing much about Elizabethan England. On the other hand, he may analyze the play for its reflection of the times without considering it as a work of art. Similarly, the works of Machiavelli, especially *The Prince*, may be read with two objectives in mind. In its pages we find Machiavelli the man who speaks for all time, and Machiavelli the former diplomat, now exiled, seeking to influence Lorenzo de Medici and thereby return to Florence.

Both approaches are fruitful. Machiavelli was indeed a true Renaissance man. He was uninterested in the rather barren religious speculation of the Middle Ages; he never wondered how many angels could fit on the head of a pin. He showed a great interest in pre-Christian antiquity. The heroes of his book are men like Moses and the leaders of ancient Rome, and not Christians of some bygone era. Indeed, Machiavelli has contempt for the Christian leaders of his own time. They seem to lack virtú, a word that appears and reappears on many pages of *The Prince*. By this, Machiavelli seems to mean that the princes of Renaissance Italy lack the ability to formulate intelligent plans and then carry them out. This ability could be found in Moses, Augustus Caesar, and other ancient leaders. It was even present in the rulers of Spain, France, and Germany. Leaders of the Ottoman Empire showed it on occasion. It is singularly lacking in the rulers of the Italian city-states, and cannot be found among the Renaissance Popes.

From this, Machiavelli draws another conclusion that again shows him to be a Renaissance man. During this period, the idea of balance engaged the interests of many intellectuals. Michelangelo shows this in many of his sculptures, especially that of David. Leonardo da Vinci's "Last Supper" is often considered a work of perfect balance, with Jesus at the center and the apostles divided equally on each side. This same sense of balance is implicit in *The Prince*. The author seems to indicate that there is a finite amount of ability in the world. At times it is concentrated in one place. Then, the world is blessed by a Golden Age of Greece or a Roman Republic. In his time, Machiavelli indicates, virtú is disseminated throughout Europe, with little concentrated in Italy. It is his hope that Lorenzo possesses enough virtú to unify and lead that sorrowful peninsula.

The anti-Christian stress to be found in Machiavelli's writings also marks him as a Renaissance Man. It should be noted that although

religious themes dominate the period, this was mainly because of
two things: (1) the worldly Church was the patron of many artists;
(2) the artists admired the beauty of the Church, but not its doc-
trines. Further, most Popes of this period were hardly religious,
and many used the office to further their personal ambitions and
those of their families. In this respect, *The Prince* represents a
challenge to the sated and weakened Papacy, and may be considered as ammunition to be used by the men of the Reformation
later on.

Machiavelli pokes fun at the Christian virtues; humility, godliness,
and charity are not to be found in his vocabulary. Instead, he uses
the vocabulary of the pagans and extols bravery, intelligence, and
the martial spirit. He scorns Christian love as a debilitating force,
and calls instead for brutality when needed. Finally, Machiavelli
has no use for heaven, the goal of the medieval philosophers. His
eye is not on the stars, but rather on the soil of a weakened Italy.
He does not chastise the Popes for their wickedness but for their
stupidity and lack of force. He is not concerned with his immortal
soul, or the world mission of Jesus, but instead writes of the need
for a unified Italy that may conquer Europe for its own sake, and
not that of a moral force. As Will Durant has written:

> The brilliant enfranchisement of the mind sapped the
> supernatural sanctions of morality, and no others were
> found to effectually replace them. The result was such a
> repudiation of inhibitions, such a release of impulse and
> desire, so gay a luxuriance of immorality, as history had
> not known since the Sophists had shattered the myths,
> freed the mind, and loosened the morals of ancient
> Greece.

But what of the lasting qualities of Machiavelli that transcend time
and place? Considered objectively and without regard to its historic
context, *The Prince* remains a great work. In it Machiavelli postu-
lates a theory of human behavior, which if not acceptable by the
prevailing morality of the time or indeed of ours, still must deserve
some respect. If one accepts his belief that man is essentially
corrupt (not very different from the dogmas of the Church), and
if one believes that man will not be called upon to answer for his
sins in the afterlife, leaving him free to pursue worldly goals, then
The Prince is a work of supreme logic. It is an attempt to deal with
the world as it is, and not as it should be. Machiavelli is not
interested in reforming human nature, but rather in using it to
serve his own ends.

He does not indicate that the unification of Italy under a Prince
who possessed virtú will bring peace and prosperity to the citizens
of the peninsula, but rather that it will increase the power of his
native land against the French, German, and Spanish invaders that
bedevil it. In this respect, at least, Machiavelli transcends time

and place. At the present time, when the force of naked power is greater than that of moral fervor, Machiavelli seems more alive than the moral preachers of the Middle Ages, and for that matter, today's believers in international order and the essential goodness of man. One cannot say that a historic figure such as Hitler was a product of Machiavelli's teachings. Hitler read and admired Machiavelli, but the Italian's conception of a Prince hardly fit the impulsive, reckless, and at times irrational German leader. Still, the century that bred a Hitler can more easily understand the philosophy of Machiavelli than almost any other.

2. Perhaps no work of the Renaissance is more quoted from than is *The Prince*. Certainly no other political scientist is referred to more than Machiavelli, whose words have become familiar to the layman as well as the specialist. For example, a recent biography of Franklin D. Roosevelt, written by James M. Burns, was entitled *The Lion and the Fox*. Extract and list some of the more familiar quotations from *The Prince* and *The Discourses*.

"One ought never to allow a disorder to take place in order to avoid war, for war is not thereby avoided, but only deferred to your disadvantage."

"Among other evils caused by being disarmed, it renders you contemptible. Because there is no comparison whatever between an armed and a disarmed man; it is not reasonable to suppose that one who is armed will obey willingly one who is unarmed."

"Wise men say, and not without reason, that whoever wishes to foresee the future must consult the past; for human events ever resemble those of preceding times. This arises from the fact that they are produced by men who have been, and ever will be, animated by the same passions, and thus they must necessarily have the same results."

"A prudent ruler ought not to keep faith when by so doing it would be against his interest, and when the reasons which made him bind himself no longer exist. If men were all good, this precept would not be a good one; but as they are bad, and would not observe their faith with you, so you are not bound to keep faith with them."

"No republic will ever be perfect if she has not by law provided for everything, having a remedy for every emergency, and fixed rules for applying it. And therefore I will say that those republics which in time of danger cannot resort to a dictatorship, or some similar authority, will generally be ruined when grave occasions occur."

"Only those cities and countries that are free can achieve greatness . . . In free countries we also see wealth increase more rapidly, both that which results from the culture of the soil and that which is produced by industry and art; for everybody gladly multiplies those things, and seeks to acquire those goods the possession of which he can tranquilly enjoy. Thence men vie with each other to increase both private and public wealth, which consequently increases in an extraordinary manner."

"I hold it to be proof of great prudence for men to abstain from threats and insulting words toward anyone, for this does not diminish the strength of the enemy; but the one makes make him more cautious, and the other increases his hatred of you, and makes him more persevering in his efforts to injure you."

"Where the very safety of the country depends upon the resolution to be taken, no considerations of justice or injustice, humanity or cruelty, nor that of glory or shame, should be allowed to prevail. But putting all other considerations aside, the only question should be: What course will save the life and liberty of the country?"

"How we live is so far removed from how we ought to live, that he who abandons what is done for what ought to be done, will rather learn to bring about his own ruin than his preservation. A man who wishes to make a profession of goodness in everything must necessarily come to grief among so many who are not good. Therefore, it is necessary to learn how not to be good, and use or not use this knowledge, according to the necessity of the case."

"I believe it to be most true that it seldom happens that men rise from low condition to high rank without employing either force or fraud, unless that rank should be attained either by gift or inheritance. Nor do I believe that force alone will ever be found to suffice, whilst it will often be the case that cunning alone serves the purpose."

"Men must either be caressed or else annihilated; they will revenge themselves for small injuries, but cannot do so for great ones; the injury therefore that we do to a man must be such that we need not fear his vengeance."

3. One of the chief considerations of Machiavelli's works is the question of morality. As we have seen, some commentators consider him to have been a most immoral man. Others claim him to have been amoral, which is to say that he thought his works had nothing to do with moral questions. A small minority of writers believe Machiavelli to have been moral. What arguments may be used to support each position?

Before discussing the question of Machiavelli's morality or lack of it, one must present an acceptable definition of the term. Most commonly, morality is thought of as belief in and practice of a set of rules or beliefs. Very often these beliefs are said to have proceeded from God. The individual who possesses such a set of beliefs and does not practice them is called a hypocrite if he realizes the disparity, and immoral if he does not. A person who lacks such beliefs is often called amoral. In addition, each society possesses what might best be called a public morality. In our society, it is considered immoral to kill needlessly, to act in a traitorous way regarding the state, to steal without cause, and to cheat. Very often commentators will note that the public morality of the West is summed up in the Ten Commandments and the Sermon on the Mount.

Historically speaking, moral codes are continually in a state of flux. While it may have been thought immoral a century ago for women to smoke or drink in public, today such occurrences are considered by many to be amoral. Similarly, George Washington was moral from the American viewpoint, but immoral from that of the British Tories. The businessman of the nineteenth century who sweated his workers may be considered moral by other businessmen, immoral by the social workers of today, and amoral by a Marxist who believes that such actions are part of the "iron law of history." The soldier who kills on the battlefield is a hero; the ex-soldier who kills at home is sentenced to death. The man who steals to feed his starving family may be considered moral; the criminal who robs a store for no apparent reason may be considered immoral or amoral.

Religiously speaking, morality may be thought of as an absolute. In other words, murder may be considered evil at all times, no matter what the reason or the cause. Even if the entire society accepts murder, and goes so far as to reward murderers, the act is nonetheless evil in the eyes of God. If such a religious figure has power, his private morality may become the public morality. Such a situation prevailed in Geneva under the rule of John Calvin and, to a more limited extent, in Puritan New England.

We turn, with this in mind, to Machiavelli's morality. If the reader believes in an absolute morality, which has been enunciated in the religious teachings of the *Bible,* then Machiavelli was indeed an immoral man, not only in his public life but in his private actions as well. He disregards all of the accepted Judeo-Christian values, often mocks them, and seems to consider those held by others as beliefs to be used, but not considered carefully for one's own use.

If we view Machiavelli against the backdrop of the Italian Renaissance, he cannot be considered immoral. When one considers the actions of the rulers of this period, one realizes that *The Prince* was as much a work of description as it was of analysis. The values and actions described in its pages were not unheard of during this period, and had Lorenzo read the book, he would have recognized his entire family and most of his friends on the pages. The difference between Machiavelli and the princes of the period lay in the fact that many of them were hypocrites, claiming to be good

Christians but acting as pagans, while Machiavelli was not guilty of this inconsistency.

If *The Prince* is viewed as a work of art, and we divorce it from the time and the place, then we may gain a truer insight into the moral questions involved. Machiavelli was unconcerned with the moral questions posed by religion, but vitally concerned with those of politics. To him, the Pope's violation of the Ten Commandments was not to be condemned, or even judged; he was immoral because he failed as a political leader. Similarly, Cesare Borgia is praised for his political consistency, while his personal morality in the conventional sense was not even discussed.

Machiavelli has a clear-cut philosophy of history and a consistent view of the nature of man. He believes that history runs in cycles, and that man can learn of future happenings by consulting the record of past events. Thus, the history of ancient Rome was being repeated in Renaissance Italy. The cycle may be God-given or natural, but this is not important to Machiavelli; for him it exists, not as a moral or immoral force, but as a cold, scientific fact. This is what he means when he says that God gives us the opportunity, but leaves it to us to make use of it. The rules of the game may be set down by a mighty lawgiver, but he does not interfere with its play. In this respect, the horror that greeted *The Prince* was similar to that which led to the condemnation of Galileo by the Inquisition. To the Church, the concept of man acting in an amoral fashion and of the heavenly bodies revolving around the sun without the intervention of God at all times was sinful, to say the least. To Machiavelli and Galileo, it merely was observable, and had no more moral meaning than the existence of a beard on a man's face.

Machiavelli, then, emerges as an amoral scientist. Popular opinion to the contrary, he did not believe that all men at all times were evil. Rather, he states, "I believe that the world has always been the same, and has always contained as much good and evil, although variously distributed among the nations according to the times." This was to Machiavelli what the law of the conservation of matter was to nineteenth century physics. And neither was considered the province of the Church.

If Machiavelli is viewed in this light, the question may be more easily answered. He possessed several well-defined beliefs, and acted on them. In his writings, at least, he was no hyprocrite. Once Machiavelli's frame of reference is accepted, and the reader rids himself of his beliefs in absolute truths, the question of morality and immorality become superfluous. Machiavelli never attempted to speak to that question in any event. To him, the important questions of power were not of a moral nature. If this can be accepted, then Machiavelli emerges as a man who rejects revealed religion, and considers all personal actions to be amoral. All, that is to say, except the unification of Italy. It should be noted that the only fervent part of *The Prince* is the last chapter, where Machiavelli indicates that any means may be used to gain this end. Because of this recurring theme, which reappears in almost all his works, we may view him as a moral fanatic on this one point. Just as Savonarola would burn the irreligious at the stake, so Machiavelli would condemn the enemies of Italian unification to the dustbin of history.

This point is not carefully made by many students of the book and the man. In this respect, it may be instructive to compare Machiavelli to Marx. Both men claimed to be scientific. Both had clearcut views of history. Each believed in a form of predestination, though neither accepted the Christian God. Marx did not consider the capitalist to be evil; rather, he was playing a role in the historic process that was preordained by historical forces, as represented in the "iron law of history." Similarly, Machiavelli thought the Prince would have to act as the agent of history if he were to succeed. Finally, one might note that each man wrote two important works: Machiavelli was the author of *The Prince* and *The Discourses,* while Marx's books were *The Communist Manifesto* and *Capital.* Few readers look into the larger and in many ways more complete works. Both men are judged by shorter, simpler statements that were geared for particular audiences and not intended as complete statements of philosophy. And *The Prince* and the *Manifesto* each end on a call to arms.

BIBLIOGRAPHY

The following are the most important of Machiavelli's works:

The Prince
Discourses on the First Ten Books of Titus Livius
The Art of War
Mandragola
Belfagor Arcidiavolo
The History of Florence
On the Characteristics of the French
Report on Affairs in France
Remarks on the Urgent Need to Raise Funds
Official Letters
Private Letters
Decennali
Report on Affairs in Germany
Seranade
Carnival Songs
Canzone
Diverse Epistles on Ingratitude
Ambition
Fortune
The Golden Ass
Discourse on Language
The Betrothed
Discourse on the Reform of the Florentine Government
Resumé of Public Affairs in Lucca
Art of Being an Ambassador
La Clizia

The following are works about Machiavelli, or deal with important events of his lifetime.

Barincou, Edmond. *Machiavelli.* 1961. This is the best short biography of Machiavelli, and stresses his writings against the background of the times.

Ridolfi, Roberto *The Life of Niccolò Machiavelli.* 1954. This is an obscure work, which will be useful only to those who already have a knowledge of the man and his times.

Strauss, Leo. *Thoughts on Machiavelli*. 1958. A careful analysis, presented in the form of lectures, on various aspects of Machiavelli's thought. Especially good on *The Discourses*.

Lewis, Wyndham. *The Lion and the Fox*. 1955. A rambling, often confusing, analysis of the impact of Machiavellian thoughts in particular and Italian ideas in general on Shakespeare and other Elizabethan writers.

Olschki, Leona. *Machiavelli the Scientist*. 1945. A short, overly-enthusiastic work of praise for Machiavelli's methods of analysis.

Vaughan,· Herbert. *Studies in the Italian Renaissance*. 1929. Contains a short, clearly-written, though conventional biography of Machiavelli.

Meineçke, Friedrich. *Machiavellism*. 1957. A reprint of a classic history of Machiavelli's impact on Western thought. At times difficult, but well worth the effort.

Villari, Pasquale. *The Life and Times of Niccolò Machiavelli*. 1892. A long, at times tedious biography of the man as set against the backdrop of Renaissance Italy. This is the most complete work on the subject, and contains material not to be found elsewhere.

Pulver, Jeffrey. *Màchiavelli: The Man, His Work, and His Times*. 1937. Clearly written, and preferable to Ridolfi.

Muir, D. E. *Machiavelli and his Times*. 1936. Contains good portraits of Renaissance Florence and some of Machiavelli's companions.

Schevill, Ferdinand. *History of Florence from the Founding of the City through the Renaissance*. Easily the best work in the field. The serious scholar should read Schevill's work before entering into those of Machiavelli.

Burckhardt, Jacob. *The Civilization of the Renaissance in Italy*. 1962. A reprint of the nineteenth century classic. This book contains valuable insights into the Renaissance mind.

Gilbert, Allan. *Machiavelli's "Prince" and its Forerunners*. 1938. This work places *The Prince* in its historical context, and makes it appear to be less revolutionary than many people believe.

Whitfield, J. H. *Machiavelli*. 1947. A clearly written but overly-simple introduction to the man and his works.

Butterfield, Herbert. *The Statecraft of Machiavelli*. 1940. Generally considered the best work on the subject.

Gooch, G. P. *Studies in Statecraft and Diplomacy*. 1942. Contains a sharp criticism of Machiavelli's methods and philosophy.

Praz, Mario. *Machiavelli and the Elizabethans.* 1928. A confused, confusing, and obscure work in the field of literary history and criticism.

Burnham, James. *The Machiavellians: Defenders of Freedom.* 1943. A defense of the doctrine by a leading conservative writer.

Cassirer, Ernst. *The Myth of the State.* 1946. Contains a perceptive analysis of Machiavelli's methods as a political scientist.

Samuel, Maurice. *Web of Lucifer.* 1947. An exciting historical novel revolving around Machiavelli and Renaissance Italy.

Prezzolini, Giuseppe. *Niccolò Machiavelli.* 1928. Well-written, but superficial.

Earle, Edward M., ed. *The Makers of Modern Strategy.* 1944. Herbert Butterfield has a brilliant short article on *The Art of War* in this book.

Mattingly, Garrett. *Renaissance Diplomacy.* 1955. Exciting and well written.

Chabod, Federico. *Machiavelli and the Renaissance.* 1950. The author analyzes Machiavelli in the mainstream of Italian history.

NOTES

ᴍ MONARCH NOTES
Available at Fine Bookstores Everywhere

ACHEBE - Things Fall Apart
AESCHYLUS - The Plays
ALBEE - Who's Afraid of Virginia Woolf
AQUINAS, ST. THOMAS - The Philosophy
ARISTOPHANES - The Plays
ARISTOTLE - The Philosophy
AUGUSTINE, ST. - The Works
AUSTEN - Emma/Mansfield Park
AUSTEN - Pride and Prejudice
BECKETT - Waiting for Godot
Beowulf
BRADBURY- The Martian Chronicles
BRECHT - The Plays
BRONTE - Jane Eyre
BRONTE - Wuthering Heights
BUCK - The Good Earth
CAMUS - The Stranger
CATHER - My Antonia
CERVANTES - Don Quixote
CHAUCER - Canterbury Tales
CHEKHOV - The Plays
CHOPIN - The Awakening
COLERIDGE - Rime of the Ancient Mariner
CONRAD - Heart of Darkness/Secret Sharer
CONRAD - Lord Jim
COOPER - Last of the Mohicans
CRANE - Red Badge of Courage
DANTE - The Divine Comedy
DE BEAUVOIR- Second Sex
DEFOE - Robinson Crusoe
DESCARTES - The Philosophy
DICKENS - Bleak House
DICKENS - David Copperfield
DICKENS - Great Expectations
DICKENS - Hard Times
DICKENS - Oliver Twist
DICKENS - A Tale of Two Cities
DICKINSON - The Poetry
DINESEN - Out of Africa
DOCTOROW- Ragtime
DONNE - The Poetry & The Metaphysical Poets
DOSTOYEVSKY - Brothers Karamazov
DREISER - Sister Carrie
ELIOT - Middlemarch
ELIOT - Silas Marner
ELIOT - Murder in the Cathedral & Poems
ELIOT - Waste Land
ELLISON - Invisible Man
EMERSON - Writings
EURIPIDES, AESCHYLUS, ARISTOPHANES - The Plays
EURIPIDES - The Plays

FAULKNER - Absalom, Absalom!
FAULKNER - As I Lay Dying
FAULKNER - Light in August
FAULKNER - Sound and the Fury
FIELDING - Joseph Andrews
FIELDING - Tom Jones
FITZGERALD - The Great Gatsby
FITZGERALD - Tender is the Night
FLAUBERT - Madame Bovary/Three Tales
FORSTER - Passage to India/Howard's End
FRANK - Diary of a Young Girl
FREUD - Interpretation of Dreams
FROST - The Poetry
GARCIA-MARQUEZ - One Hundred Years of Solitude
GOETHE - Faust
GOLDING - Lord of the Flies
Greek and Roman Classics
Greek and Roman Classics
GREENE - Major Works
HAMMETT - The Maltese Falcon/Thin Man
HARDY - Far from the Madding Crowd
HARDY - The Mayor of Casterbridge
HARDY - Return of the Native
HARDY - Tess of the D'Urbervilles
HAWTHORNE - House of the Seven Gables/ Marble Faun
HAWTHORNE - The Scarlett Letter
HELLER - Catch-22
HEMINGWAY- A Farewell to Arms
HEMINGWAY - For Whom the Bell Tolls
HEMINGWAY - Major Works
HEMINGWAY - The Old Man and the Sea
HEMINGWAY - The Snows of Kilimanjaro
HEMINGWAY - The Sun Also Rises
HESSE - Siddhartha
HOMER - The Iliad
HOMER - The Odyssey
HUGO - Les Miserables
HUXLEY - Major Works
IBSEN - The Plays
JAMES - Portrait of a Lady
JAMES - The Turn of the Screw
JAMES - Washington Square
JOYCE - Portrait of the Artist as a Young Man
KAFKA - Major Works
KEATS - The Poetry
KESEY - One Flew Over the Cuckoo's Nest
KNOWLES - A Separate Peace
LAWRENCE - Sons & Lovers
LEE - To Kill a Mockingbird
LEGUIN - Left Hand of Darkness
LEWIS - Babbitt
LOCKE & HOBBES - The Philosophies

(Continued)

(Continued)

LONDON - Call of the Wild
MACHIAVELLI - The Prince
MARLOWE - Dr. Faustus
Marxist & Utopian Socialists
MELVILLE - Billy Budd
MELVILLE - Moby Dick
MILLER - The Crucible/A View from the Bridge
MILLER - Death of a Salesman
MILTON - Paradise Lost
MOLIERE - The Plays
MORE - Utopia
MORRISON - Beloved
Mythology
The New Testament
The New Testament
NIETZSCHE - The Philosophy
The Old Testament as Living Literature
O'NEILL - Desire Under the Elms
O'NEILL - Long Day's Journey into Night
O'NEILL - The Plays
ORWELL - Animal Farm
ORWELL - 1984
PATON - Cry the Beloved Country
PLATO - The Republic and Selected Dialogues
POE - Tales and Poems
POPE - Rape of the Lock & Poems
RAWLINGS - The Yearling
REMARQUE - All Quiet on the Western Front
Rousseau & the 18th Century Philosophers
SALINGER - Catcher in the Rye
SALINGER - Franny & Zooey
SARTRE - No Exit/The Flies

SHAKESPEARE - Antony and Cleopatra
SHAKESPEARE - As You Like It
SHAKESPEARE - Hamlet
SHAKESPEARE - Henry IV, Part 1
SHAKESPEARE - Henry IV, Part 2
SHAKESPEARE - Henry V
SHAKESPEARE - Julius Caesar
SHAKESPEARE - King Lear
SHAKESPEARE - Macbeth
SHAKESPEARE - The Merchant of Venice
SHAKESPEARE - A Midsummer Night's Dream
SHAKESPEARE - Othello
SHAKESPEARE - Richard II
SHAKESPEARE - Richard III
SHAKESPEARE - Romeo and Juliet

SHAKESPEARE - Selected Comedies
SHAKESPEARE - Sonnets
SHAKESPEARE - Taming of the Shrew
SHAKESPEARE - Tempest
SHAKESPEARE - Winter's Tale
SHAKESPEARE - Twelfth Night

SHAW - Major Plays
SHAW - Pygmalion
SHAW - Saint Joan
SINCLAIR - The Jungle
Sir Gawain and the Green Knight
SKINNER - Walden Two
SOLZHENITSYN - One Day in the Life of Ivan Denisovich
SOPHOCLES - The Plays
SPENSER - The Faerie Queene
STEINBECK - The Grapes of Wrath
STEINBECK - Major Works
STEINBECK - Of Mice and Men
STEINBECK - The Pearl/Red Pony
SWIFT - Gulliver's Travels
THACKERAY - Vanity Fair/Henry Esmond
THOREAU - Walden
TOLKEIN - Fellowship of the Ring
TOLSTOY - War and Peace
TURGENEV - Fathers and Sons
TWAIN - Huckleberry Finn
TWAIN - Tom Sawyer
UPDIKE - Rabbit Run/Rabbit Redux
VIRGIL - Aeneid
VOLTAIRE - Candide/The Philosophies
VONNEGUT - Slaughterhouse Five
WALKER - The Color Purple
WARREN - All the King's Men
WAUGH - Major Works
WELLS - Invisible Man/War of the Worlds
WHARTON - Ethan Frome
WHITMAN - Leaves of Grass
WILDE - The Plays
WILDER - Our Town/Bridge of San Luis Rey
WILLIAMS - The Glass Menagerie
WILLIAMS - Major Plays
WILLIAMS - A Streetcar Named Desire
WOLFE - Look Homeward, Angel/Of Time and the River
WOOLF - Mrs. Dalloway/To the Lighthouse
WORDSWORTH - The Poetry
WRIGHT - Native Son
YEATS - The Poetry
ZOLA - Germinal

PRENTICE HALL